Making the Most
of Your Placement

Making the Most of Your Placement

John Neugebauer and
Jane Evans-Brain

Los Angeles | London | New Delhi
Singapore | Washington DC

SAGE Publications Ltd
1 Oliver's Yard
55 City Road
London EC1Y 1SP

SAGE Publications Inc.
2455 Teller Road
Thousand Oaks, California 91320

SAGE Publications India Pvt Ltd
B 1/I 1 Mohan Cooperative Industrial Area
Mathura Road, New Delhi 110 044

SAGE Publications Asia-Pacific Pte Ltd
33 Pekin Street #02-01
Far East Square
Singapore 048763

Library of Congress Control Number: 2009921296

British Library Cataloguing in Publication data

A catalogue record for this book is available from the
British Library

ISBN 978-1-84787-567-9
ISBN 978-1-84787-568-6 (pbk)

Typeset by C&M Digitals (P) Ltd, Chennai, India
Printed in Great Britian by CPI Antony Rowe, Chippenham, Wiltshire
Printed on paper from sustainable resources

To our families

Anne, John and Ruth

Robert and Bethan

Contents

Acknowledgements

In preparing this book, we have drawn both on our own knowledge and experience with working with students and graduate development but we have also researched with a wide range of universities, placement organisations, and, most of all, students themselves.

Many people gave us their views and encouragement by being interviewed for the book, and reading early drafts. We wish to thank everyone who supported, facilitated, inspired, or informed us during this process. With such a wide range of people involved, it seems unfair to pick out individual contributions, but also wrong not to acknowledge those who have particularly given valuable time to help us. So thanks to Faith Pilgrim, Sophie Runcorn, Sue Johnstone, Susan Jackson, Leanne Glide, Heather Collier, Paul Thomas, Ross Hovey, Dorothy James, Clare Jeffries, Katie Leak, Thomas Lamb, Paul Hammond, Kristina Lau, Thomas Brown, Sian Paley, Maria McCabe, Maria Feenan, John Charles Neugebauer, Jacqueline Smith, Erkan Hassan, Libby Beck, Jim Wood, Karly Crewe, Sidonie Flook, Edel Conway, Nathan Redshaw, Alexandra Mottram, Rhys Bevan, Sue Durbin, Rachel Skew, Professor David Clutterbuck, Jane Measures, Heather Jones, Duncan Greenman, Alysha Morgan, Libby Beck, Donna Miller, and Charlie Leake, and all the individual students, universities and organisations contributing to research for the book.

We would also like to acknowledge the support and encouragement from our publishers, SAGE, and particularly to thank Kate Wood and Clare Wells for their patient and professional support as we moved from concept to final manuscript for the book, and the anonymous reviewers for their helpful comments and suggestions.

Every care has been taken to ensure the current accuracy of information, but information which is right one day can quickly become out of date, or may not be applicable to particular individual circumstances. Neither the authors nor the publishers can accept responsibility for the current accuracy of information contained in the book and you are strongly advised to check current conditions from the sources we have signposted in the book.

Chapter 1

Introduction

Chapter contents

1.1 About this study guide

So you are thinking about doing a placement or an internship? If you manage this opportunity well, it will help both your academic success, and your future career prospects. This book has been written for undergraduates and postgraduates who have already planned, or are considering, a placement or internship as part of their courses. It has been written based not only on the authors' personal experiences of working in organisations with university students, but also after research with a selection of universities, organisations, and students themselves. It has been designed to help you whether you are doing a specialist course requiring a placement, or a more general course, which may not even require a mandatory placement of internship.

Getting the most from your placement is not just about finding somewhere to work for a year, but also about making the most of the learning opportunities which this will present. So this study guide will take you through finding, undertaking, and learning from a work placement or internship. To do this, the book is divided into the following sections to reflect the different stages of placement.

Introduction

Chapter 1 is an introduction to placements – what they are, and why you should think carefully about whether a placement is right for your studies, and longer term career.

Section 1

In Chapter 2, we will give further guidance on how to find a placement, and, in Chapter 3, how to apply. Being shortlisted for a placement opportunity is one step nearer success, but you need to make sure that you maximise your chances in interview and in assessment centres. So in Chapter 4, we explain how to prepare for interview, group assessments, presentations, and the battery of tests which you can expect at assessment centres. In Chapter 5, we look at the important not-so-small print – tax, work permits, and what to do if you plan to work abroad for your placement or are a visitor to the UK.

Section 2

For many placement students, settling into a new organisation can be very different from the student or vacation employment experience. In Chapters 6 and 7, we discuss the practical steps of settling into your new organisation, and outline your employment rights and obligations. To support your learning and development in your placement, Chapter 8 explains how you can make the most of learning opportunities generally.

Section 3

It can be easy to think that university is somehow in another world, once you are in an organisational work role, and particularly easy to slip by or be 'too busy' to start academic work, especially if you have a dissertation to complete. In Chapter 9, we provide advice on planning and delivering your dissertation, and ensuring that you set aside sufficient time for this.

Section 4

And so after all the preparation and hard work finding and doing your placement, it is over. If you are still not sure whether or not a placement is right for you, or where or how long that placement should be, Chapter 10 closes this guide with the accounts of three actual students' stories about their placements. They discuss what went well in their placement, the challenges they faced, and what they would have done differently.

1.2 The wider picture of graduate job prospects

For many organisations, engaging student placements and internships is not just about offering development opportunities for students, nor even about getting work done. Although these are both important, placements will often be an integral part of the organisation's graduate recruitment process: organisations using this approach may recruit 70–90 per cent of their graduates in this way. But even where graduate recruitment is not part of an organisation's objective, universities, organisations, and students themselves can testify to the value a placement brings to longer term job applications, and a renewed enthusiasm and application to university studies.

> ## Why organisations offer work placements – some examples of what employers say about their views of a successful placement
>
> - A student who is willing to become fully immersed into the organisation and relevant department(s). For example, our current placement student has been carrying out testing on a new software system, this is a business critical system and his input has been valid and appreciated. (Financial Services Company)
> - Referral for a conditional job offer on graduation at the conclusion of the placement. (LloydsTSB)
> - We consider direct applications – so it is important that applicants research us in advance, and clearly show how they could achieve development with us, as well as giving something to the organisation … Placements must not be about photocopying or making coffee – so we find a role with tangible outcomes, such as in a project, or in research. (Zurich Financial Group)
> - Placements are a very valuable experience. With new ideas and up to date skills, we learn as much from them as we hope they learn from us. (UK Border Agency)

It has been estimated that approximately 29 per cent of UK students undertook some form of internship during their final two years of study (Universum, 2006). But this lags behind our closest European Community competitors where 66 per cent of German students and 79 per cent of French students undertook some form of internship. It is little wonder, therefore, that UK Regional Skills Partnerships include Graduate Placement Programmes as part of their Higher Education and Higher Level Skills objectives (see, for example, South West of England Regional Development Agency, Graduates 4 Business).

Students who have completed a placement or an internship are more likely to obtain a good degree than students of similar ability without a placement. And students who have worked on a placement and achieve a 2.2 degree are as likely to find graduate level careers as students with a 2.1 degree who have not completed a placement. So a placement has a double benefit in helping you to find a graduate level job, and in obtaining a higher degree classification.

But irrespective of the chances of improving your course marks, the value of a good placement or internship is in helping you to understand better the type of work you wish to do, and with whom you wish to do it.

The key is how to make the most of your placement and internship opportunities – finding the best placement opportunities, competing to get a place, and making the most of the learning, development and networking opportunities your experience offers. This book has been written in the chronological order of the placement process to help you navigate through each stage of the placement process.

We take you through all steps of your internship and placement, step by step, from search, application, placement itself, to making the most of your placement afterwards too. The book draws on hints and tips from students who have been through the process already, research with a selection of universities, and research with organisations themselves.

Think back to how long, as a student, you prepared for university. For a few, the idea of a university place may have been quite late into the final years of school, or have even come after school. But for most students, planning and preparations for university start three or four years previously: in choosing the right subjects, building CVs, and starting to think about the right courses and locations for your studies.

If you have chosen a course with a placement or an internship, it makes sense that similar care and thought need to be given to choosing the right placement, and making the most of it. Your placement year is likely to be very different from work experience you may have had as a student, as one student commented:

> The change from a part-time job in a shop to my placement is astounding! ... it can be lonely and very difficult at times.

But despite the challenges, the vast majority of students would summarise their placement experiences in the same way as this student:

> Definitely do a placement. It will really boost your confidence and your capabilities.

The key is for good preparation and personal management whilst on your placement.

The first question to consider is whether a placement is for you. What are the benefits of deferring completion of your studies, and if you do so, how do make the most of it?

In 2007, the Association of Graduate Recruiters estimated that, on average, 29 graduates were chasing each graduate vacancy, and that for some organisations, the number was as high as 104 per vacancy. But UK employers frequently bemoan the fact that graduates do not have the necessary skills. Why?

Despite the improvement in degree classes, and the wide availability of specialist and general courses, employers regularly say that graduate applicants lack the *skills* and the *competences* they are looking for. For example, in 2008 *People Management*, the professional journal for HR specialists, suggested that two thirds of UK graduates lacked adequate communication and interpersonal skills, and 54 per cent lacked leadership and managerial skills. In a conference launching the Confederation of British Industry's Higher Education Task Force, employer representatives said that more than a fifth of employers were dissatisfied with graduates' soft skills, communication, and self-management. One representative was even more blunt – saying that students needed to 'get up in the morning'.

You may have your own views about the validity of these opinions and statistics. Business dissatisfaction about graduate readiness for employment is not just a twenty-first century gripe – for example, in the eighteenth century, Adam Smith wrote in *The Wealth of Nations* that:

> The greater part of what is taught in schools and universities does not seem to be the proper preparation for business. (1819: 361)

So this is the job market which you are entering as a graduate. And history suggests that it won't change much by the time you graduate! One student explained it this way:

> When you first go to university, you are under the illusion that once you graduate, you will be swamped by job offers because you have a degree to your name. However, by talking to other people you will soon realise the struggles you will incur to find this employment after graduation without having the experience in the field you want to go into. Recognising the need to gain this experience whilst studying I looked into gaining a work experience placement.

Universities themselves recognise that students need to develop employability skills. As one commented:

> A placement is very important to students nowadays as degrees are becoming more commonplace. The only thing that differentiates a student in the graduate market (especially in degrees such as business studies or marketing) is relevant work experience. Other than that, students are very small fishes in a very big pond.

There is also a wide and increasing realisation within work organisations of the value of work placements. Research by Heaton and colleagues pointed to the 'vital importance that was attached to the placement experience' (2008: 283). As examples, they quote the views of HR managers who actively use placement students as part of the graduate development process:

> We definitely prefer to recruit students who have completed a work placement. In fact completion of a work placement as part of a degree gives applicants a big advantage since we select through assessment centres, using competency based criteria. The work placement means that applicants have more experiences to draw on. But once they are with us, those with work placement experience are less unrealistic than those without (HR Manager, Engineering Organisation). (2008: 282)

> Those having completed a work placement have hands-on experience of technical aspects – those who don't, may know what to do in theory, but they don't have the confidence to do it in practice (HR Manager, Construction Organisation). (2008: 283)

So the case in favour of doing a placement or internship is strong. To make the most of your degree and future career, improving employability skills will lift you above the competition and improve your chances of getting the role you are looking for. Placements and internships are a great way of improving these all important employability skills ... and helping you decide what you want to do in the long term as well.

Why employers use work placements and internships

Research by the National Council for Work Experience shows that employers see the benefits which well thought-out placements can bring to their companies in terms of:

- Gaining an intelligent, motivated, cost-effective labour resource with valuable skills, knowledge and fresh ideas.
- Flexibility in availability (students may be available at times of the year when the need is greatest).
- Projects being undertaken that would otherwise require valuable time from fulltime employees or where the relevant skills are not in place.
- Permanent staff gaining opportunities to develop supervisory skills by mentoring and monitoring placement students.
- Recruitment and training costs being cut by employing placement students when they graduate.
- Temporary staff shortages being overcome at low cost.
- It being a 'taster' session for both parties with no commitment.

Source: National Council for Work Experience (2008). Reproduced with permission.

1.3 What are placements and internships?

One newspaper article described the difference between work and a placement like this:

> Work means moaning about the boss, drinking tea, and helping yourself to the stationery cupboard – all while getting paid. Work experience means being enthusiastic, diligent, and full of ideas, whilst not receiving a penny. (Swain, 2008)

By the time you complete your placement, we hope that you will have a more positive view! Work placements are not necessarily unpaid, but what are placements and internships? We will use the two terms interchangeably.

The key features of a placement or internship are:

- Placements and internships may be undertaken during your first degree, after your first degree, as part of professional training, or as part of postgraduate studies.

- The appointment is always for a fixed period. It may be for as little as one or two weeks, and typically up to 12 months.

In a placement, you will be expected to work, but it is generally recognised and accepted that you are also there for training and experience purposes. So, at times, you may find yourself 'shadowing' a more experienced colleague – for example, attending meetings, as an observer. You may attend more learning events than some of your colleagues; or gain wider work experience in the organisation. At other times, you may be involved in the day-to-day activities of the organisation; or perhaps working on specific one-off projects. Just sometimes, you may even find yourself with not enough to do.

You may find that your work is assessed in a slightly different way from more permanent colleagues. You may be subject to a different performance and potential assessment process within the organisation, using formats which have been specifically designed for graduates or placement students. Your placement employer may be asked to submit a report on you in your university's format; or, in rare cases, there may not be a report on you at all. If you are on a placement, it is very important to know how you will be assessed, and we say more about this in Chapter 4.

You may be paid during your placement, or, for short-term placements, you may not receive any pay at all. The national minimum wage does not apply if your placement is part of your university course.

Unlike many of your permanent colleagues in your placement organisation, you may also be required to undertake university work, such as planned assignments, keep a learning journal or learning log, or research projects or dissertations. This is an essential part of your learning, and will add considerably to your workload. As well as developing your research, analytical, and interpersonal skills, this will also represent a key time in developing your ability to manage potentially competing demands and priorities. To guide you through this, in Chapter 8, we will help you to understand why reflective learning is considered to be so important, and how to develop your capabilities as a reflective learner; in Chapter 9, we discuss how to tackle your dissertation.

1.4 Why you should consider a placement

A placement will represent a break from your university, or current job, so is a key investment in the future. Therefore the arguments for and against doing this need to be thought through carefully, especially if the placement is for 3–12 months duration.

Short placements

Shorter placements, for example during your summer vacation, may be less intrusive on your university studies, but are still time consuming. These short placements – 'trophy placements' – may look good on your CV, but are relatively low impact in developing your competences and experiences. The shorter the placement, the less likely it is that you will be paid, especially in some highly popular graduate employment destinations, such as media roles. Nevertheless, even short placements can give you some experience and demonstrate to future employers your initiative, commitment, and drive to succeed in your chosen area. Perhaps most importantly of all, any placement gives you the opportunity to extend your network, to understand what you may wish to do in the future, and to have a clearer idea of what to do to achieve your aspirations.

Longer term placements

Longer term placements of 3 months, 6 months, or 12 months are most likely to make a real difference to your employability skills, and to be formally integrated into your study programme. Just as important, they are more likely to be paid as well!

Careers after graduation

As we have seen, the hard fact is that organisations often seem to have a poor view of graduate employability skills. During your placement, you will better understand the types of competences and skills which employers are looking for, and how to develop graduate level examples of competences and skills. As a result, you will be more able to compete for jobs when you apply for them on completion of your studies. Equally, your work placement will have given you a better idea of the types of job which are most likely to interest you, and the sorts of organisations you are likely to prefer.

The arguments in favour of internships and placements apply equally well if the placement is a mandatory part of your degree studies, or if you are studying more academic subjects, such as the humanities. In both cases, you are developing the skills and competences for your future career, developing networks, and establishing a clearer sense of those areas which you want to develop further, or avoid altogether.

Similarly, students who have completed placements have found themselves more motivated to work well, better organised in their work, and more able to see the linkages between the theory they are taught at university, and its practical application. The universities recognise this too, and one university placement manager commented:

> On return to university, students tend to do very well academically due to a stronger work ethic, a greater understanding, clearer goals, better time management, and an ability to get up early.

The workload is higher if you opt for a placement, but also makes more sense because it feels more 'joined up' and relevant. A placement will often help you to choose your final year options as well.

Placements not directly linked with a university course

Many students are now leaving university with no real idea of what they want to do, or without a track record to pursue their aims. As a result, applying for career roles can be an energy sapping and demoralising experience. Short-term placements/internships may be especially useful for this group – whether during vacations from a university course, or even following graduation.

However, whilst this group may still have access to university careers advice, getting a placement, and maximising the learning from it, can be more challenging. Yet, the principles of this book are just as valid as if the placement was part of a university course.

University studies

More organisations are saying, at least publicly, that a degree classification is less important than someone having the right work competences and skills. Alternatively, they may say that they will still consider graduates with weaker than expected degree results. For some organisations, it may be true that they give genuine and full consideration to graduates with less than 2.1 degrees. However, in order to compete with the large number of graduates seeking graduate employment, any weakness in your application needs to be avoided if possible. As we have already seen, placements will help to lift your overall course marks, and may also take you into a higher degree class.

Why a placement? Some student views

- I chose this degree ... because it enables me to carry out a placement year. I believe that this is essential [in] applying my theoretical knowledge, whilst gaining invaluable experience in industry ... more than just a paper based education.
- I thought that it would give me a wealth of experience ... help me to decide what to do on graduation ... hoped that one of my placements might lead me into a job or at least a field of interest.
- I hoped that the placements would make me more employable as I would likely have more and better experience than many peers at similar universities with similar degrees.
- To get real life experience so that I can enhance my CV in order to get a better graduate job.
- My placement will help me to collect information for my dissertation.
- To gain a better degree.
- ... The increased likelihood of finding employment after graduation. Prospective employers know a student who has experience of industry will need less time to fit into the culture of work and that the student will also have had first-hand experience of applying many of the skills and techniques learned at university to 'real world' problems.
- The course included a compulsory placement year, which was the deciding factor in choosing my university ... the experience gives you an excellent advantage over other students when you graduate.
- It is the ideal time to look outside and discover the type of work and environments that I enjoy, and more importantly what I don't. I feel that it will enhance my understanding of how theories and techniques I study at university are used in the workplace. I firmly believe that this type of study can only enhance my final year grade.
- I would advise anyone to do a placement. You get so much experience, you gain new experience, you gain new skills that you never thought you could, you meet new skills, and you get a taster of what life will be like after you graduate. Finally, you get a jump start ahead of the graduates who did not do an industrial placement.
- To enhance my understanding of how the theories and techniques I study at university are used and adapted in the workplace.

For some students, the decision to take a placement year was not taken until after the start of the degree course:

- When I started my course, I hadn't intended to do a placement ... I just wanted to do a three year degree course. But during my first year, I went to presentations on placements. They showed that you had a much better chance of a better job and a better degree if you did a year out. I am pleased with my decision to do a placement.

1.5 When a placement may not be such a good idea

For some people, and some courses, a long-term placement may not be a great idea, so this needs some extra thought.

Previous experience

If you have come to university having already had substantial work experience, and especially experience in the area you plan to apply for after university, then a long-term placement may not be right. Alternative strategies could include:

- Making sure that you stay in touch with your former place(s) of work, including any short-term vacation employment.

- Short term placements (1–2 weeks are ideal) in organisations or roles in which you may be potentially interested. With reasonable luck, your previous work experience will mean that you can settle in quickly, and make a positive impression, despite the short time frame. The other advantage of the short placement is that, with good personal organisation, you may be able to experience more than one organisation, and so develop a wider network of roles and organisations.

- Volunteering, either during term time, or during vacations. Volunteering may be of particular value if you are looking for a future career in the not-for-profit sector. It may also provide valuable experience in a range of professionally related roles such as teaching support, media, law, care, communications, etc. And don't forget, any volunteering helps to develop your work skills, shows your initiative on your CV, and underpins your interpersonal skills during assessment processes.

Professionally based degree courses

For some professions and occupations, you may be better advised to complete your degree as soon as possible, and then join a professional training scheme. Here too, a planned approach to short-term placements during your university career will help to convince potential employers of your initiative, and that when you apply to them for work, you are doing so with the benefit of a well informed choice regarding your organisation and role preferences.

An academic career?

Alternatively, you may be certain that you want an academic career and have the strong academic results to justify this choice. Again, it may be better for you to continue with your degree, get an excellent result, and move on to a higher degree. But remember also that a placement may give you a very important insight into organisational life, which could be important if your subsequent research requires you to do fieldwork in outside organisations. It also helps you to hedge your bets in case you change your mind on your career choice, or do not achieve the grades to enable you to do a higher degree.

1.6 Large organisation or small?

A placement is not just about making you a better employment prospect, important as that is. It also represents a great opportunity for you to see the kinds of jobs, organisations, and work environments which you may enjoy in your future career, or, on rare occasions ... never want to see again!

Should you look for a placement in a large organisation, or a smaller one (often referred to as SMEs – Small to Medium Sized Enterprises)?

A big organisation may look good on your CV, but remember that the role you have, and the learning you get from it, are more important. Larger organisations may offer a wider range of job roles and might back up extensive advertising of placement opportunities with generally well designed placement schemes. They may also have more sophisticated assessment and support for placements than a smaller organisation, and must be a clear favourite if you want to work in a large organisation on graduation.

Smaller organisations may be harder to find for a placement, but once you have located one willing to take on a placement student, there may be less intense competition for a place than in larger organisations, especially outside the major cities. If you find the right placement, you may gain much wider experience than in larger organisations. This can give you a better opportunity to develop your skills and competences, and so your future marketability. Indeed for some disciplines, working in small organisations or specialist agencies may be the best way to develop networks for your future career choice.

Just as important as the size of the organisation you join for your placement is the manager you will be working for and the work you will be doing. If possible, ask if you can meet your manager during the selection assessment process. This is usually easier to arrange in a smaller organisation, but less likely to be practical in a larger organisation.

Which organisation? Some student views

- I mainly wanted to get a job in a large organisation so that I could get experience of a big company.
- I looked at a range of organisations from placements in manufacturing to ones in commerce and finance.

- Organisations which have tried and tested placements ... I knew I would not [want] to be a guinea pig as the first placement student.
- I wanted a company that cared for their employees and customers ... not just making a profit. The company [I chose] is very ethical, with a great reputation for employee development and ploughing back their profits into schemes to benefit the local community.

But for other students, the type of role being offered was more important than the organisation:

- The role sounded great, and I could gain lots of experience in different areas.
- I looked at organisations that could offer me all-round experience ... the ability to work in different departments ... I felt this would help me in the future.
- Working in a communications team differs from [my current] computer course, so I am able to gain skills that will benefit me later in life.

1.7 Home or away?

The organisation and job that you go for are probably more important than where you may want to live, but it is still important that you will be comfortable with where you will be living. Many placements are based in London or the major cities. They provide attractive prospects, but do make sure you work out your budget for travel, accommodation, sport, a social life, and your general living expenses first! However, do not overlook placement opportunities outside the large cities, especially if they are close to your home or university. In some cases, employers find it more difficult to fill placement opportunities here, and so, as well as saving money from working nearer home, you may find that the competition is less intense as well.

Alternatively, you may have the opportunity to work overseas. Finding a suitable role is likely to be more difficult, as the organised channels which make this possible in the UK may not be so clear cut for overseas jobs. You are more likely to find an overseas placement if you already have contacts in your chosen country, for example, through your university, or via friends or family abroad, or perhaps by following up contacts from previous years' students.

[My placement gave me an] understanding of research and development in the pharmaceutical industry and experience of a full-time job. I also completed a research project which was good practice for my final year research project. Improved my German, made many friends and travelled a lot in Europe. (UK pharmacology student on placement in Switzerland)

Overseas work and placements require more planning and more active management than UK placements. A well organised and successful overseas placement will be great for your CV, personal development and future employability. But the risks if you get it wrong are obviously higher than for the UK. Before you board that plane, make sure that your needs and expectations are consistent with those of your proposed host organisation. Domestic issues are also more complex if you go abroad, and so we cover these in more detail in Chapter 5.

1.8 Timeline to success

If you are planning a longer term internship or placement, you will need to prepare well in order to make the most of the opportunity. The timeline below has been prepared to help you with this, and is the ideal span you should take to prepare yourself – if you have less time available, you can still get ready, and follow the advice here. Shorter internships (one week to one month) will not need so much detailed planning, but the timeline will still give you some ides about the questions you should be asking, and the follow-up action to make this a meaningful part of your university learning.

Placement timeline

18–12 months ahead (see Chapters 2–4)

- Update your CV to be a generic CV.
- What type of organisations are likely to appeal to you, and why?

  - Read business or professional press articles and job applications for a better idea of the job market.
  - Check with the university placement/careers service.
  - Speak to family and friends for a clearer idea of work experiences.
  - Discuss with students who have been through work placements, or who are currently applying for roles.

- Think about short-term placements/internships now, even if these are 5–10 days and unpaid.

12 months ahead (see Chapters 2–4)

- Attend university briefings on placement opportunities.
- Set up and maintain a file/folder with all the material relevant to your placement preparations.
- Check carefully with professional bodies for information on expected work experience and skills, and on Continued Professional Development (CPD) requirements.
- Update (again) your generic CV.

- Understand how you would demonstrate the relevant competences and skills in a targeted CV/application by completing the competence example table.
- Check the closing dates for applications amongst larger organisations.
- Prepare and submit targeted application letters, CVs, and applications.
- Plan how you will develop key skills in group work and presentations.
- Practise numeracy, verbal reasoning, and similar psychometric tests.
- Be ready for telephone interviews and web-based assessment tests.

6 months ahead (see Chapters 3–4)

- Apply now to smaller organisations for placements.
- If going abroad, check and follow up all visa, health, insurance, accommodation arrangements.
- To help with dissertations, etc., double check remote access to university information and library services, including journal access; check whether/how you may be able to use library services in other towns and cities under university library reciprocal arrangements.
- Get constructive feedback on your applications/assessments – don't be fobbed off by generalisations – what did you do well/not so well? Use this to develop future assessment strategies.

Placement period (see chapters 5–9)

- Settle in to the organisation!
- Buy, and use, a diary for short-, medium-, and long-term planning – use the year planner to scope your dissertation plans.
- Start and maintain your own Personal Development Plan.
- Use a learning journal to make notes on what you have learned that week.
- Reflect on key learning – what has gone well, not so well, and why.
- Be clear about what is expected of you: work objectives; how the organisation may expect you to develop skills and competences; university requirements.
- Find one or two mentors to help guide and support you.
- Network.
- Make sure that you have details of who (and how) future employers can contact future referees in your host organisation, which is especially important if your placement has been outside the UK.

Post placement (see Chapter 10)

- Update your competence example table and ensure that your generic CV is fully up to date and includes new examples of your achievements during your placement.

(Cont'd)

- Volunteer to speak to the induction group for the next intake of students in your host organisation; or to potential placement students back at university.
- Register your Continuing Professional Development papers with your future professional body if appropriate.

Hints and tips from students, universities, and placement organisations

- Start thinking about a placement early ... at least 18 months ahead.
- Apply early – for one year placements, large organisations often fill most of their roles in the autumn *before* the autumn you plan to start. So it is not too early to start making sure that your CV and application details are up to date during the summer after your first year.
- Even if you had not previously thought about a placement, find out more when you start your university course.
- Placements are not for you? Then still pay attention to developing your employability skills during your university course through volunteering, short-term internships, etc.
- The quality of ideas (and applications) is more important than quantity.
- Whilst it is best to start early, don't give up! Even attractive and popular organisations may still be filling placement roles in the early summer to start in the Autumn.
- Don't give up either on applying for short-term placements in popular organisations (for example, the BBC). If you want to get experience, keep applying.
- Smaller organisations often leave it quite late before filling placement vacancies. Some may not even have a programme, but can be so attracted by the quality of your approach and enquiry that they follow it up with a discussion.
- If your applications are regularly ignored or rejected, double check that they are well presented, and then be patient. It's not personal. Think how many publishers rejected J. K. Rowling's Harry Potter!

1.9 Summary

A work placement during your academic studies will help you link theory and practice to your studies. It is likely to help you to get a better degree, and to shape your future career and organisation choice.

Finding the right placement will take time and will also be competitive. As with graduation, you will be competing for jobs with similarly qualified people. Start planning for your placement early, and be perseverant in getting the right organisation for your needs.

The upside here is that your placement is a great opportunity to work, continue to learn, and develop your CV. There will be few times in your working life when you will have such an opportunity to learn whilst you work. Every work situation is likely to have its ups and downs, but very few placements are a total disaster. The key is to see all your experiences as developmental – in this way you will exploit your placement to the full. This book has been prepared to help you navigate your way through your placement, and will give you detailed advice to fast track you through the learning curve. So good luck and Make the Most of Your Placement!

1.10 Further information

There is a wide range of reading material to help you decide what you want to do, and where you might do it. Here are some starter ideas:

National Council for Work Experience
www.work-experience.org
For a wide range of information and contact points.

Prospects
www.prospects.ac.uk
For information and sources on graduate job opportunities.

Family and friends
A great source, often under-exploited, of wisdom, opportunities, ideas, networks and contacts. Let a wide circle of people know that you are going on a placement, even a year ahead, and see what ideas come up! Don't forget also to speak to students who have recently returned from placements.

Overseas scholarships
Some organisations exist to promote trade and national links through exchange and internship programmes. For example, take a look at the

Mountbatten Scheme (www.mountbatten.org), which provides internship opportunities in the USA.

University Careers Office; University Placement Office
Be best friends with them! Make sure that you attend organisation briefings and take advantage of interview and assessment centre skill development workshops if these are available.

Rate my Placement
www.ratemyplacement.co.uk
Students' views on experiences in a wide range of organisations and a site for possible placement opportunities.

Working Abroad
www.workingabroad.org
For ideas and information on overseas internships and volunteer roles.

Conferences and Exhibitions
Keep your eyes open in quality newspapers and through web searches for conferences and exhibitions, organised both for placements and graduate opportunities. It is worthwhile to go to graduate recruitment fairs and meet prospective employers, since the representatives doing graduate recruitment will often be the same people responsible for placements. Talk to the people on the stands to find out any information which may not be given in their brochures (e.g. what percentage of placements are offered full-time roles, what is their attitude on UCAS points or degree class, etc.).

Checklist

1 Start early!
2 Use the timeline in this chapter to get ready.
3 Start thinking early – is a placement right for you? Where would you like to be? What kind of role might you want? Talk with family and friends, and to people who may have already done a placement.
4 Thinking of going abroad? Start planning now, and have a UK fallback in case the overseas placement applications do not work out.
5 Visitor to the UK from abroad? Check that you have all the required documentation and permissions to do your placement in the UK (Chapter 5).
6 What support and advice is available from your university?
7 Talk to students who have recently returned from university about their experiences.
8 Attend university presentations on placements.

Section 1

Getting a Placement

If you aim to get a placement whilst at university, this section will help you to navigate the opportunities, challenges, achievements and some frustrations and disappointments in the process.

So, in **Chapter 2 Finding a Placement**, we give you some advice on how to find those placement opportunities, using well known, and some less well known, techniques.

Whilst many students may have had experience of applying for part-time work, the selection for placement opportunities is usually much more demanding, and may often be as structured as full graduate recruitment processes. In **Chapter 3 Applying for Roles**, we take you through different application processes and how you can present your personal information in a way which is most likely to attract organisations. In **Chapter 4 Interviews and Assessment Centres** we explain how to prepare for selection processes and give some tips on how to make the most of the actual day.

There are important legal requirements which you must comply with in your placement, especially if you are receiving benefits, or working internationally. In **Chapter 5 The Important Not-so-Small Print** we outline the main issues which you should be looking for and point to where to go if you need additional help.

Chapter 2

Finding a Placement

Chapter contents

2.1 Why organisations offer placements

Organisations themselves have a variety of motivations for offering student placements – as additional support, as a way of developing learning in the organisation or a recruitment pool for graduates, and even for more highly principled reasons such as developing the next generation of entrants with appropriate work skills.

The Lambert Review (2003) of business–university collaboration highlighted the importance of business helping to develop entrepreneurship and business awareness through placements. Furthermore, it showed that 59 per cent of employers had said they provided work experience or placements for graduates in 2007, and that 22 per cent would be prepared to increase their number of placements (CBI/Pertemps, 2007). So in principle, there will be places for everyone who looks for a placement, even though very many organisations do not actively advertise that they take placement students.

The example over the page is based on a discussion with the European HR Director for Enterprise Rent-A-Car.

Placement scheme – Enterprise Rent-A-Car
In discussion with the European HR Director

Why do it? What does Enterprise get from it?

There are many benefits that Enterprise receives from our intern programme. The key reason is talent. By having a placement programme in place, we have access to students early. We promote our programme to first and second year students, whilst some companies only select second year students. This opens the door for us to get access to these students, and ensures that we are not missing out on this talent.

We offer very flexible options for students ranging from summer to year round placements. Many of our interns continue working part-time when they return to university. Again, this gives us the opportunity to keep them in our pipeline – and to keep them busy and not interested in other employers.

Recruiting interns into our business also helps us operationally over the busy summer months. And because many of our interns want to continue working for Enterprise once the scheme ends, they will continue to work part time and during the holidays.

We have a number of our interns who apply for campus brand manager roles with us. This also embeds them further into our culture. Because the students already interact with departments, lecturers and student organisations, these brand managers can quickly build relationships and influence others. For the students, it's a fantastic opportunity to put 'serving in a leadership role' for Enterprise Rent-A-Car on their CV, and they can also make a bit of cash in the process.

We do offer our successful interns places on our graduate scheme for when they complete university. We do this at the end of the second year of their placement. This further cements our relationship with them – and they can get on with enjoying their final year and not having to worry about searching for a job.

How many interns are taken on permanently?

We currently take 80 per cent of interns into our full-time graduate management scheme. The good news is that whilst the students are on the placement scheme, the time that they spend with us counts towards their time in the management role. So, if a student spends a year with us, it's possible that they will complete the management trainee role and qualify to become a management assistant. And when they return post graduation, they don't begin again as a management trainee – they go right into a management assistant role and hit the ground running.

How do students apply?

Interns take on the very same responsibilities as our management trainees. They will get hands-on and classroom experience from the very first day. Interns learn about sales, marketing, customer service, business management and operations. And the expectations for performance are at the same level. Therefore, we use exactly the same application process for our intern programme as we do for our management trainee scheme. This is a combination of an online application, face to face interviews and an assessment centre. Throughout the interview process, we look at the same competencies which we know will give the intern a good chance of becoming a permanent fixture with Enterprise once they graduate.

2.2 What organisations look for in placement students

It is an important thought although somewhat depressing – that, at a national level at least, employers' representatives such as the Confederation of British Industry (CBI) see problems with the quality of students in the job market. As a potential placement student, you need to understand these perceived shortcomings, as it will give you the opportunity to present your application more strongly. Table 2.1 shows where it is that employers believe graduates need stronger skills.

This is a useful benchmark for understanding what you can do individually to improve your preparations for placement, how to present your

Table 2.1 Areas where employers are dissatisfied with graduates' key skills

Skill	Employers expressing dissatisfaction
Foreign languages	54%
Business awareness, satisfaction and loyalty	48%
Self-management – accept responsibility	36%
Enterprise/innovation/creativity	27%
Generic employability skills	27%
Knowledge about chosen career	26%
Basic literacy and use of English	26%
Positive attitude towards work	21%
Basic numeracy skills	17%

Source: CBI/Pertemps, 2007

application, and how to develop your employability whilst you are on a placement, so as to maximise your job seeking opportunities when you do graduate. We will focus on how you can do this later in the book.

So what do individual organisations look for as they recruit placement students? In the box below, we show a selection of the academic disciplines and competences which a selection of organisations say they look for in placement students. Of course, this is only a sample of a few organisations, and different organisations will have different requirements. But the two key messages to take from this sample are:

- Organisations are rarely prescriptive about which degree you are studying, although specialist roles do require specialist degrees, and there is a tendency to prefer business studies subjects for commercial roles. According to the CBI, employers put greater emphasis on generic employability skills than a specific degree subject, with the result that about 70 per cent of advertised graduate jobs do not specify a degree subject (CBI, 2007: 20).
- Far more important are the competences which organisations look for – team work, delivering results, ability to learn, customer orientation, and so on. We will discuss in Chapters 3 and 4 how to demonstrate these competences, but it is essential that you can provide evidence from your previous experience in these areas.

What placement organisations are looking for

Each organisation has its own requirements for placements, but here are some of the key things which organisations have told us they particularly want to see when appointing placement students:

National Supermarket Chain (Somerfield)

Academic disciplines: We decide the department for the placement first and then decide on the relevant academic background, which generally doesn't need to be precise.

Competences: Individual backgrounds and knowledge are less important for us. What we really want are drive, energy, and a willingness to learn and succeed. An understanding and appreciation of great customer service is also key.

Financial Services Company

Find out about the placement organisation before you apply and go for an interview. We always ask candidates what they know about us. Some of them seem to know more about the company than we do which is obviously impressive.

Global Energy Company (BP)

Academic disciplines: Our placements may cover 17 different disciplines. For some, such as engineering and sciences, we look for specialised courses. For our commercial placements, including HR, finance, and purchasing, we pay more attention to the student than specialist academic qualifications.

Competences: All placement applications are then assessed on thinking ability; working together; business sense; influencing skills; personal drive; and technical excellence in the area to which they have applied for a role.

LloydsTSB

Academic disciplines: We encourage applications from all degree disciplines, choosing to focus more on the skills and behaviours a candidate demonstrates. For us, a clear motivation and understanding of the area applied to is essential. For Corporate Markets, a financial discipline such as maths, economics or finance is a pre-requisite.

Competences: We look for judgment, drive, influence and execution where leading teams to deliver, showing sound decision making and a clear motivation are key.

Global communications (BT)

Academic disciplines: For technical roles, we generally recruit from a computer sciences-related subject; for more commercial roles, we recruit from any discipline, but these do tend to be business focused.

Competences: Customer focus; communication; and team working skills.

Savings, Investments, and Insurance organisation

Academic disciplines: A business-related degree is most relevant for this sector.

Competences: Customer focus; teamwork and interpersonal skills; self development; integrity.

Global Aerospace Manufacturer

Academic disciplines: Broad-based subjects for business-related areas, and specialist engineering degrees for engineering placements.

Competences: Team work behaviours are essential; proactive; good self-organisation.

UK Border Agency

Academic disciplines: no preferred subject for 70 per cent of graduate roles.

Competences: Self-management; team working; business and customer awareness; problem-solving; communication and literacy; application of numeracy.

2.3 When to look for a placement

There are few 'rules' for when to start looking for a suitable placement, other than to start early (12–15 months before your planned placement period), and never to give up!

For long-term placements in larger organisations, make sure that you start your search, and your applications, as early as possible since many larger organisations work on placement recruitment in the autumn before the autumn they expect placements to start. However placement vacancies will still be available in the few months prior to the actual start dates.

For medium-term placements (say, three months), a shorter application process is normally expected. However, if you are considering a placement in a popular area (such as book, media, or web publishing) do be prepared for strong competition if you are proposing to do a 'stand alone' placement over the summer vacation.

Short-term placements (one–two weeks) are usually unpaid, but if you can afford the time (and cost) these are great ways to get an insight into your target organisation/role/profession. You may be able to arrange a short-term placement without too much previous notice, especially if this is through a direct approach to the organisation or a networked contact. Once again, however, there are no strict rules for this, and some organisations with highly popular short-term internships (for example, the BBC) may look at placement applications many months in advance of their actual requirements. Also, like holiday bookings, short-term placements may be easier to organise outside of obviously popular periods, such as university summer vacations – if you can be flexible on dates, you may be more likely to be successful with short-term applications. Applications for short-term placements will often have a short shelf life – if you haven't heard anything within two to three months, then assume that you are unsuccessful: if you are determined to get in, have another look at your application and then reapply.

University advice on finding that placement

- A placement is a structured learning experience – not just a contract of employment. So make sure that your placement will give you learning and development opportunities.
- Unless you are working in a very competitive industry, don't be tempted by unpaid or poorly paid placements.
- Don't think of yourself as 'the placement student' – you can make a huge contribution so don't undervalue yourself.

Advice from the National Council for Work Experience (NCWE) on finding and securing a placement

Whether you are looking for a year's internship as part of your course, or a few weeks work during the holidays, here are a few tips for securing that all important placement which may give you the edge in the graduate job market.

- Attend the National Work Placement Exhibition every October and November.
- Look at websites, for example, Graduate Prospects has a search placement facility.
- Make use of various newspapers.
- Use your careers advisory service – they can offer a wealth of experience on work experience, and can also advise on where to find the work experience you are interested in as well as helping to tailor CVs and covering letters to give you the maximum chance of success.
- Do your homework – find a company you would like to work for and check out their website. Companies like applicants to show that they have done their homework on the business.
- Presentation – first impressions count! Turning up for an interview in jeans and trainers is unlikely to impress. An interview is your chance to sell yourself so dress for success.
- Timing is everything – spring and summer are good times to apply speculatively as employers will be considering how to cover staff holidays – you might well be the perfect person to fill the gap.
- Look for organisations with recognised programmes, for example those with an NCWE Work Experience Award or Quality Mark accreditation.

2.4 What you want to gain from a placement

Try to think about your placement as more than 'something you have to do', and really think proactively about what you want to get out of it. For example, we have already seen in Chapter 1 that organisational size does not necessarily mean a better quality placement, since smaller organisations may give you more variety and responsibility than larger ones; smaller organisations may also be preferable if you are doing specialised work.

Similarly, think about the type of role you want. Do you want a specialist role to enhance your specialist or professional knowledge (for example in IT, law, finance, the media, or engineering), or a more generalist one to gain a more widespread understanding of how a business runs?

Think also about the competences (Chapter 3 and 4) and skills (see later in this chapter) which you already have, and still need to develop for when you have finished your studies. If you have a specialist career in mind, then working on specific areas of technical, specialist, or professional practice may be best. If you still are uncertain about your future career, then a general route is usually better.

Student placements preferences

- [*Student on a 2 × 6 month placement scheme*] I chose HSBC because I liked the roles they were offering and thought it would look good on my CV. My second placement was with [a smaller organisation called] Astellas. I chose this job as something I would really enjoy, and because I had a good feeling about the company and the job. Having worked at HSBC ... I was looking for a smaller company, and felt that I would benefit from this experience and enjoy it more.
- I mainly wanted to work in a large company so that I could get experience in a big organisation. I also wanted to work in a big organisation on my CV, and hoped that I could work for this organisation in the future.
- I started looking at organisations which might be fun to work with – [organisation names withheld] ... But then I began to realise that whilst they may look attractive on the outside, when thoroughly researched, they would not be particularly beneficial to me in terms of self-development and graduate opportunities. I then started to apply to companies which had a strong focus on personal development and good graduate opportunities.

2.5 Where to look

The sources of information on placements (and subsequent graduate careers) are generally under-exploited as suggested in Figure 2.1 below. Here, we will look at the range of sources of information which you should consider in your search for a placement.

University placement service

Your university placement office is the obvious starting point for most placements and to advise you. Not only will they have great contacts with organisations who have worked with them successfully in the past, and thus will have a good idea of the number, type, and culture of the organisation, but they will also be liaising with managers who will tend to be familiar with the type of student they will get, and any assessment and in-service work

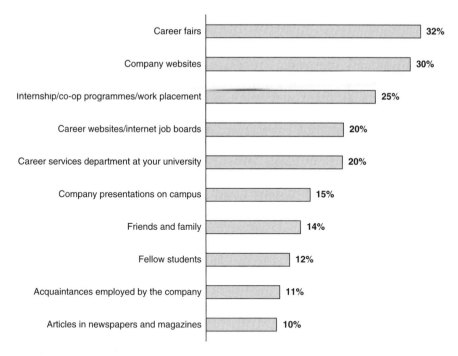

Figure 2.1   **Sources for finding graduate/placement opportunities for UK university students**

Source: Universum, 2006. Used with permission.

requirements. Your university placement office wants you to succeed, and is well equipped to help you do so.

A minority of students reported that their placement offices either seemed to want to push students in a particular direction, or wanted to vet placement organisations before giving approval for the placement. Remember, however, that your placement office wants you to succeed. The placement office is much more likely to be able to help you if you have done some initial research and preparation, and can articulate what it is that you want to achieve from your placement.

'Skiing off-piste'

Organisations may prefer to take students from particular universities. In limited cases, this is because they genuinely believe those students are the 'best quality' for them. But in most cases, they work with a limited number of universities simply because it is administratively easier to handle relationships with those universities. So, if you find that an organisation takes placements/ internships, but is not on the list of available placements at universities, and you are convinced that you would like to apply to them, then do so!

Graduate careers and placement conferences and fairs

These are great places for improving your understanding of opportunities, timescales and requirements. Graduate careers fairs will tell you about some of the organisations in the market for graduate job opportunities, and may give you a few leads for placement opportunities as well. Placement fairs give more precise targeting to organisations who are looking for placement students, and some of these will also be using placement students as part of their graduate recruitment processes. These fairs also have short workshops and presentations on application processes, and so can help you to become more street wise in how to apply. But don't forget that these fairs are only a small snapshot of the range of opportunities available that you can get out and search for.

Web searches

These are also a great way to start your search and to see some of the placement opportunities available. Again, this helps you to understand what is out there and the role requirements, but don't forget that there will be many other organisations – often the smaller ones – who would welcome a placement student, but have not advertised on websites.

Direct application

Direct applications can involve a high number of enquiries to a limited number of successful follow-ups. But even if an organisation is not advertising a placement or internship it may still welcome an application, especially for short-term internships. According to the Employment Trends Survey (CBI/Pertemps, 2007) the key here is to have researched the organisation, and to be clear about what you can offer that organisation and what you would like to achieve from a placement. You are more likely to be successful, if you:

- Have already networked with someone in that organisation, through earlier work experience, a job fair, social meeting, etc.

- Have researched the organisation's website (where there is one), so as to have a clearer picture of their activities, how they prefer to handle job vacancies and applications, and, by looking at current vacancies which they may be advertising, how they describe competences and skills relevant to that organisation.

- Can address your application to a named individual in the organisation.

- Ensure that your targeted CV is accompanied by a short letter of application (see Chapter 3).

- Follow up with a telephone call, three to four weeks after your initial enquiry.

- Remember that it is debatable whether a posted letter or email is more likely to be successful.

Networking; family and friends; previous employers; other students

Make sure that family and friends know that you will be looking for a placement, and start this process 15–18 months ahead of when you want to begin your placement. The two reasons for doing this are to gather views and ideas about places to work, and what you might expect, and to exploit any direct or indirect contacts which may lead to further ideas on a good placement, or more directly to a placement opportunity.

Overseas placements and internships

These may be amongst the most attractive for some students in terms of personal development. But despite the clear learning and development benefits of working abroad, there are practicalities which also need to be considered. Overseas placements are usually difficult to organise unless you already have clear and established contacts abroad (for example, through your university). Also, once abroad your placement may also be more difficult to manage, so this requires a good level of independence and resilience on your part. Finally, if you are considering your placement as a potential direct entry route into a graduate level job with a particular organisation (rather than as a learning experience in its own right), a UK placement may be preferable. (See also Chapter 5.)

2.6 Updating your employability before placements

As well as applying for suitable placement opportunities, you are strongly advised to ensure that you update your skills so as to make the most of your placement, once you start it.

Think about the types of skills which your placement organisation may be looking for and then plan how you will close any gaps. For example, how comfortable are you at making presentations? If the answer is 'not very', then this is a good time to become better prepared. Use the skill self-assessment audit in Table 2.2 to look at the types of skills you will need in the workplace and how you may improve them, and then plan what you will do to make sure that you are ready.

Not only will it help you to update your skills prior to selection and placement, it will also be of benefit when you are working and will boost your study skills on your return to university.

Table 2.2 Skill self-assessment audit

Skill	Typical employer requirements	You may need to do more preparation if you ...	Development ideas	Your personal action plan – what will you do personally to develop these skill areas?
Time keeping	Arrive at meetings and at work on time! Deliver required work on time, even if this means you need to put in extra effort, time, or research.	Are usually late or unreliable for lectures, seminars, etc. Hand in work on time.	Get into the habit of keeping a diary. Plan longer term work, and break it down into milestones, noted in your diary.	
Work prioritisation	Deliver required work on time, even if this means you need to put in extra effort, time, or research.	Find it difficult to balance workloads, e.g. skip seminars to meet hand-in deadlines for other subjects.	Step back and think why this is happening. Do you have too much on, with too many competing demands? Or are you not using your time as effectively as you should?	
Numeracy	Non-specialist roles: able to undertake simple percentage, fractional, adding and subtracting calculations; able to undertake more	Have had little practice using numeracy skills since GCSE, little practice using numeracy skills on spreadsheets	Practise now. You can buy a test book or do tests on line.	

Table 2.2

Skill	Typical employer requirements	You may need to do more preparation if you ...	Development ideas	Your personal action plan – what will you do personally to develop these skill areas?
	complex calculations using spreadsheets; able to draw accurate tables, graphs, etc. using software, and interpret results intelligently.			
	Specialist roles: if your subject has more advanced numeracy, mathematical, or statistical requirements, ensure that you are fully competent in these.			
Writing	Write straightforward reports and correspondence using appropriate structures, grammar, spelling and punctuation.	Have difficulty planning and writing university assignments.		
	Ability to prepare short reports and letters to a brief or with minimal guidance.			

(Cont'd)

Table 2.2

Skill	Typical employer requirements	You may need to do more preparation if you …	Development ideas	Your personal action plan – what will you do personally to develop these skill areas?
Presentation	In work and assessment, make a presentation in a professional manner, take questions, deal with some resistance/ hostility from the audience.	Little or no experience of presentations; reluctant to volunteer for presentations in seminars, unfamiliar with using flip charts and PowerPoint (including computers) for presentations.	Become actively involved with society or tutorial presentations. Read Chapter 4 which has tips for improving presentations. Join university societies which give you opportunities to speak in public, or perform (drama, music, etc.).	
Self-motivation/drive	A competence more than a skill. But employers look for an ability to work to deadlines without constant supervision, and to show initiative as required.	Skip seminars, lectures, and sports training or practice sessions. Fail to do required reading for seminars.	Not easy to learn from a course or a book. Set yourself goals, write them down, check how often you have achieved or ducked them. Discuss with a mentor.	
Computer skills	Fully competent in all major programmes, including Word, databases; spreadsheets; file management.	Most students cope well with Word packages. How comfortable are you with spreadsheets, preparing graphs, using databases, etc.?	Find somewhere to take the European Computer Driving Licence qualification; your university may do this as an extra-curricular course.	

2.7 Further information

Many websites provide further information on placements, including opportunities overseas. Here is a selection of those available at the time this book went to press. But remember also that many organisations, especially smaller businesses, may not advertise their placement opportunities – so find out about these and contact them directly.

National Council for Work Experience
http://www.work-experience.org/ncwe.rd/index.jsp
The essential first visit site to get your bearings on placements and a gateway to many ideas and possibilities.

AIESEC
http://www.aiesec.org/cms/aiesec/AI/index.html
AIESEC offers a wide range of international opportunities, conferences, and exchanges ... and serves as an agent of positive change through education and cultural exchange to develop a broader understanding of cultural, socio-economical and business management issues. Go to their website and see the wider range of student opportunities available internationally.

GO Wales
http://www.gowales.co.uk/
Great selection of placements graduate opportunities, and more, in Wales.

Shell STEP Summer Placements
www.step.org.uk

United Euro Bridge
http://www.unitedeurobridge.org
A voluntary organisation which aims to improve the availability of placement opportunities for students across Europe.

Ideas for Placements
www.doctorjob.co.uk/workexperience
www.justjobsfor4students.co.uk
www.fledglings.net/
www.milkround.com

Internships in the USA
www.aipt.org/

Europe
www.iaeste.org.uk/students.htm

Checklist

1 Undertake an honest self-assessment of your current skills levels, and decide on how you can develop and practise these ahead of your applications and selections.
2 Start thinking about what kind of role you want and the reasons for this. Specialist to develop professional skills, or generalist to give you a taste of different aspects of organisational life?
3 If you are thinking about going abroad for your placement, start looking early on and be realistic (see also Chapter 5 for information on the practicalities).

Chapter 3

Applying for Roles

Chapter contents

3.1 Organising to succeed

Preparing for your placement, and finding the right one for you, will take at least as much time as finding your first university place. So you must organise yourself adequately to deal with your placement/internship search methodically – remember, your placement is likely to be a highly formative experience for your future career.

Think of yourself as an employment brand: what is it about your personal qualities that would encourage an organisation to invest further time in you? To prepare for this, you will need to be very clear about how your skills and competences fit with your prospective organisations' requirements, and how you will present this information both in your interviews and in your CV.

3.2 Competences and skills

How organisations will assess your capabilities and worth will vary greatly, depending on which sector of the economy they are in, their own selection and assessment processes, and the size of the organisation.

But despite these variations, a key approach which many organisations will adopt is to consider your competences to fill the required role. This is an important difference from those at university, where it is usually your theoretical knowledge which is tested. Many candidates will be weak at organising and presenting examples of their competences. On the other hand, some organisations may also have a mindset that placement applicants, and, in particular graduate applicants, do not have sufficiently well developed competences for their roles. This level of poor self-organisation from the applicant, and predetermined mindset from organisations, may contribute to organisations' perceptions that universities do not turn out graduates with 'the right job skills'.

So, a clear understanding of competences is essential to support your application. In the workplace, you will be required to show that your role-related competences are developing – and in seeking graduate level opportunities, your applications will be stronger if you can articulate your competences well.

Therefore, in this chapter, we will explain:

- What competences are.

- How you can prepare and make the most of your competences when applying for roles.

In Chapter 4, we will explain how employers assess your competences at recruitment, and what you can do to make the most of this part of your assessment.

In Chapters 6–7, we will consider how to plan for and develop your competences in the workplace, so as to make the most of your placement, but also to position you for your future career roles.

What are competences?

Competences have been defined as

> the behaviours that employees must have, or must acquire, to input into a situation in order to achieve high levels of performance. (CIPD, 2008)

They may also be referred to as competency and competencies – for the purpose of job applications, the two words can be used inter-changeably.

Organisation priorities for competences

Research undertaken by the CIPD (2008) and other research bodies (for example, Rankin, 2004) suggest that organisations usually rate the following competences in order of priority:

1 communication skills (interpersonal and written skills)
2 people management
3 team skills
4 customer service skills
5 results-orientation
6 problem-solving.

You should be aware, however, that these are generic topic names. In many cases, an organisation will rename competences so they fit more closely with the internal language, business and culture of that organisation.

Early applications of competence frameworks were mainly focused on performance management and development, particularly of more senior staff. Today, however, it is generally recognised that an effective competence framework has applications across the whole range of human resource management and development activities.

Competence frameworks are now seen as an essential vehicle for achieving organisational performance through focusing and reviewing an individual's capability and potential. Moreover a competence framework can be a key element in any change management process by setting out new organisational requirements. Similar findings also emerged from the 2004 IRS survey (Rankin, 2004).

How you can prepare and make the most of your competences when applying for roles

Organisations may want to consider your experience – practical illustrations of what you have done previously. But for placement students (and graduate recruitment), many will recognise that they can train you and give you the relevant experience. So what they are looking for instead is that you have the right competences. In Table 3.1, we show what competences are, and the types of question which you might be asked.

You need to be able to demonstrate your competences (and the potential for these) both in your CV and in interviews. Table 3.2 has been designed to help you review the strengths and development areas in your competences and skills. You should complete this in preparation for your applications, and prior to interviews.

Keep Table 3.2 up to date and use it to highlight competence examples in your CV or covering letter. It will also be useful to prepare competence examples prior to interviews.

If you only have weak examples in some competence headings, think how you can fill these gaps in the time before you apply for placements. Use these examples for telephone and web-based interviews and try to remember these examples for face-to-face interviews.

3.3 Organising your CV

… or, more appropriately organising your CVs, since you will need more than one version of your CV for applications.

Your CV and covering letter need to be excellent, and it will take time to get these right. Even so, you need to know here that your application will receive only scant attention at a first sifting. The reader will not spend very long looking at it – you will have a couple of minutes, at best, to convince them to put you in the 'To see' pile, rather than the reject pile. So the CV which that employer receives must look as 'right' as possible for that organisation. The

Table 3.1   Competences: typical interview questions

Use this table to prepare for competence-based interviews. Put your own examples of working with these competences in Table 3.2. When you answer competence questions, use 'I', not 'we' – to explain *your* contribution. Practise interviews in advance.

Typical competence headings	Typical positive example questions	Typical negative example questions
Excellent customer service	How do you ensure excellent service to customers? Tell me about a time when you have provided extra effort to deliver excellent service.	Tell me about a time when you have failed to deliver excellent service, and what you did about it.
Team working and team leadership	How do you work with other members of the team? How do you work with a team when you are supervising team members?	When have you had difficulties working with a team member? How did you resolve this? When have you been the source of a problem in the team? How did this happen?
Delivering results	How do you make sure that you deliver what is required of you? When have you delivered results above expectations? How did you do this?	When have you failed to deliver something which you had previously agreed to do? How did this happen?
Problem solving	Give me an example of how you have resolved a work-based problem.	When have you faced an insurmountable problem?
Innovation	Give me an example of when you have used creativity and innovation to resolve a work-based problem. How do you innovate new approaches to the way you do your work? How have you introduced innovation in a rule bound environment?	When have you found it difficult to convince others to accept your ideas to do something new or different?

Table 3.1

Typical competence headings	Typical positive example questions	Typical negative example questions
Planning and organisation	How do you prioritise your work?	When have you had clashes of priorities? What caused these and how did you resolve them?
Integrity	How important is it for you to work in an area that is consistent with your values?	When have you had to 'bend' the rules to deliver good customer service? When have you been asked to do something which has clashed with your own values?
Ensuring diversity	How do you ensure that the work you do balances the needs of diversified groups of people?	When have you been asked to work in an environment which may have clashed with your beliefs and values in diversity?

Table 3.2   Competence example table

Having seen the typical areas where organisations may ask you about your competences, now use this table to prepare short examples of how *you* have demonstrated these competences at work, in clubs and societies, or in your studies.

Competence heading	Positive examples where you demonstrated this competence (six brief examples)	Negative examples of competence and how you recovered (three brief examples)
Providing excellent customer/client service		
Team working and team leadership		
Delivering results		
Problem solving		
Innovation		
Planning and organisation		
Integrity		
Ensuring diversity		
Managing health and safety		
Your Skills:		
IT?		
Communication?		
Other relevant?		

best way to do this is to have a general CV, and then to refine it to an individual organisation's requirements when you send in your application.

Therefore the first CV should be a general CV. This will contain all the information relevant to your education, work, and life to date. It may be quite long (three to four pages) and remember that you will never submit it to an organisation: it is only written as an overall databank for your application CVs.

Your application CVs are those that have been prepared, and tailored, for the organisation to which you are applying. The application CV stresses your suitability for that organisation by tailoring your profile so that it meets the target organisation's requirements as closely as possible. The application CV is prepared largely by cutting and pasting from the general CV, together with some final editing where appropriate. The application CV should NEVER be more than two sides long.

What to include on your CV

Your CV needs to reflect you as an individual, rather than looking as if it has been produced from a CV software download, but there are some conventions you should follow. The example on the next few pages shows a CV format and is annotated to highlight those key aspects which you should focus on with your own CV preparation.

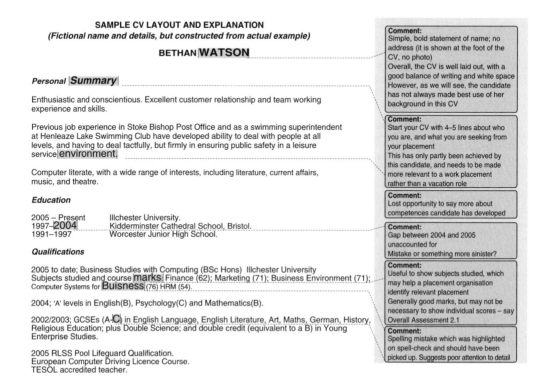

SAMPLE CV LAYOUT AND EXPLANATION
(Fictional name and details, but constructed from actual example)

BETHAN WATSON

Personal Summary

Enthusiastic and conscientious. Excellent customer relationship and team working experience and skills.

Previous job experience in Stoke Bishop Post Office and as a swimming superintendent at Henleaze Lake Swimming Club have developed ability to deal with people at all levels, and having to deal tactfully, but firmly in ensuring public safety in a leisure service environment.

Computer literate, with a wide range of interests, including literature, current affairs, music, and theatre.

Education

2005 – Present   Illchester University.
1997–2004   Kidderminster Cathedral School, Bristol.
1991–1997   Worcester Junior High School.

Qualifications

2005 to date; Business Studies with Computing (BSc Hons) Illchester University
Subjects studied and course marks: Finance (62); Marketing (71); Business Environment (71); Computer Systems for Buisness (76) HRM (54).

2004; 'A' levels in English(B), Psychology(C) and Mathematics(B).

2002/2003; GCSEs (A-C) in English Language, English Literature, Art, Maths, German, History, Religious Education; plus Double Science; and double credit (equivalent to a B) in Young Enterprise Studies.

2005 RLSS Pool Lifeguard Qualification.
European Computer Driving Licence Course.
TESOL accredited teacher.

Comment:
Simple, bold statement of name; no address (it is shown at the foot of the CV, no photo)
Overall, the CV is well laid out, with a good balance of writing and white space. However, as we will see, the candidate has not always made best use of her background in this CV

Comment:
Start your CV with 4–5 lines about who you are, and what you are seeking from your placement
This has only partly been achieved by this candidate, and needs to be made more relevant to a work placement rather than a vacation role

Comment:
Lost opportunity to say more about competences candidate has developed

Comment:
Gap between 2004 and 2005 unaccounted for
Mistake or something more sinister?

Comment:
Useful to show subjects studied, which may help a placement organisation identify relevant placement
Generally good marks, but may not be necessary to show individual scores – say Overall Assessment 2.1

Comment:
Spelling mistake which was highlighted on spell-check and should have been picked up. Suggests poor attention to detail

Employment Experience

Summer 2005 and Summer 2006 Swimming Superintendent, Henleaze Lake Swimming Club
Duties included:
Ensuring safety of swimmers in the water, and around lake club. Receiving club members, ensuring membership up to date, and taking entrance fees for guests. Lakeside Health and Safety equipment; cleaning public areas and toilets; removal of refuse; maintaining Accident and Incidents book; processing guest payments; premises closure. Reason for leaving: completion of seasonal contract.

> **Comment:**
> Candidate has skilfully buried some mediocre results at GCSE with good results. Organisation unlikely to notice or bother to follow up

> **Comment:**
> This list shows a candidate willing to get involved and with a variety of responsible roles Candidate should have made more of the competences used – customer services; problem solving; attention to detail; leadership

2004 Part time singer at the Social Club, Ilchester

Semi professional singer with house backing group.

> **Comment:**
> Make relevant to placement by mentioning competences – developed self confidence; working in teams, etc.

2002–2004 Bishopston Village Post Office

Sole charge in the afternoon/evening of the confectionery/ lottery section of the shop. Provide customer services in local community; cash up at end of day; premises closure at the end of day; security report for manger. Reason for leaving; closure of the Post Office.

> **Comment:**
> Responsible and important role. But point ruined by incorrect spelling of manager, which had not appeared on spell-check, and not noticed here either Poor attention to detail, again

2002; 2 ×1 week work experience with Lloyds TSB, Bristol

I have also undertaken voluntary work, especially at Redland Park United Reformed Church with youth group activities.

> **Comment:**
> Helpful to say why changed roles

Interests

> **Comment:**
> Say more about this
> Link with teamwork skills

Music/singing	National Youth Choir of Great Britain.
	Worcester Schools Chamber Choir.
	City of Worcester'Girls Choir.
	Played Alto saxophone at concerts and musical productions.
Theatre	I enjoy visiting theatre productions in Bristol and Ilchester.
Sports	Rowing (Ilchester Trent University Boat Crew); Tennis; Badminton; Swimming.
	Played hockey for my school.
Writing	Written articles, interviews, and reviews for my university magazine.

Positions of Responsibility/Voluntary Activities

- Tutor group representative for English and social psychology, Nottingham Trent University.
- At Kidderminster Cathedral School, I was School Council representative.
- Social Secretary for the Tennis Club.
- Voluntary activities have included:
  working in the Kidderminster Hospice shop, Whiteladies Road.
  support worker for disabled delegates at BBC media events.

> **Comment:**
> Interests do not demonstrate strong business commitment so more detail could be added here to show relevant competences and interests for the prospective placement organisation

Contact Details

2 Alder Way, Bishopston, Worcester, W12 E34
Home 0123 456789
Mobile 0987 654321
E mail Bethan.watson@myinbox

> **Comment:**
> Put these at the end. Do not use valuable space on the initial impact of your CV with administration details

> **Comment:**
> If you have a colourful or whacky email address, switch to something more conventional

Chiumento, a leading UK HR consultancy for talent development and job searching periodically surveys what employers and recruitment agencies would prefer to see on CVs. Their findings on the best use of CVs and covering letters are as follows:

- 96 per cent of employers want a two-sided CV; only four per cent of employers prefer a single page CV.

- Email is the preferred communication channel.

- CVs are best presented in Microsoft Word.

- Less than 10 per cent of employers wanted to see a photograph with the CV.

- The most immediate reasons for rejection of CVs are poor presentation, lack of clarity, low relevance for the role applied for, typos in the text, grammar errors, and inappropriate length.

- The covering letter may not be quite as essential as the CV, but you still need to get it right. It needs to be brief, but must also show how your competences and skills meet the organisation's requirements. Once again, it needs to be tailored for that organisation.

Chiumento's top 10 tips for CVs (reproduced with permission)

1 Stick with a two page CV.
2 A reverse chronology is preferred.
3 Create a strong personal profile (a short personal summary at the start, about four lines long, and focused on how you meet the requirements for that role, and not full of generic and unsubstantiated value statements.
4 Be conventional – photos, coloured paper, fancy fonts, and humour are likely to lead to rejection.
5 Highlight your achievements to be a winner – show how these are quantified (for example, grades or other measures of how you did in work-based roles).
6 Don't over-inform. Not a life history, but as a minimum, you should include a work history, any achievements, education and qualifications, accountabilities in jobs and what you achieved, plus your contact details (including email and mobile phone).

7 Make your CV stand out with words like 'I' (not 'we'), and include numbers, values, costs, profits, and so on to boost this further.

8 Be clear, accurate, and appropriate – use good grammar and no spelling, typo or grammar errors.

9 Email your CVs wherever possible. Make sure you use the right key words, as many organisations use software to pick up the key attributes they are looking for.

10 Support your CV with a high quality covering letter. Why are YOU the right person for THIS organisation?

3.4 Applications

Your application for a placement may be submitted:

- Online (especially for larger organisations);

- Via paper-based application forms, or the submission of your CV;

- Speculatively via email or a paper-based application or via your CV.

In each case, you will need to be highly organised ... and patient ... because submitting a well presented application is time consuming.

Many organisations will only accept applications if they are presented on their official application forms, whether online or on paper. The different formats used mean that applications will take longer to complete. But you can help yourself by ensuring that your general CV has all the information you will need on it already, so you can copy and paste the most relevant sections onto your application.

Covering letters, online applications, managing your personal details in Word

Below is a sample of a speculative enquiry letter for a placement. This should be short and to the point, focused on what you the applicant can offer – and what you hope to achieve in a placement.

Dear Miss Owen|

Work Placement Opportunities

I am a second year undergraduate student at Illchester University, where I am reading for a degree in mechanical engineering, with business studies. Having researched a number of organisations in which I am interested, and where I feel that I could make a contribution to the organisation as well as learn, I am writing to enquire whether you have a work placement vacancy for the period 5 September to 5 February.

I believe that I could offer|the following competences|and skills to my placement organisation:

Team work

Customer orientation

Delivering results

Skills

Problem solving

Technical and academic: please see my enclosed CV for further details, including the subjects which I have studied, and my results.

Within my placement, I am especially looking for a role where I can develop my skills| working on engineering projects, especially where there is a client focus. I believe that my general background and team working skills will be of use in this area, and will also help me to achieve my learning objectives from my placement.

I do hope that you may have a role for which I may be considered, and look forward to hearing|from you.

Yours sincerely

Comment:
The writer has taken the time to find a named person for the letter (or email) This will improve the chances of success, even with a speculative enquiry

It also gives the writer an opportunity to follow up the letter with a further email, or telephone call – say in 4 weeks – if there has been no reply

Comment:
Organisation is pleased to see the applicant focused on 'what I can offer you'

Comment:
The student has written competences and skills using a generic format

This helps the organisation to see whether the applicant has the types of competences it is seeking

The competences examples are based on the framework shown in this chapter

Comment:
Applicant is clear and specific on the types of role which would be of greatest interest

Other candidates may be more general. But remember that organisations are more likely to look at you if you can articulate what you want from the placement – and if they do not have what you want, then it is better to look somewhere else for the experience

Comment:
Our applicant has actually made a diary note to send a follow up email – or telephone call – to Miss Owen in 4 weeks time. Whilst this risks rejection, at least the applicant knows if there is any chance of an interesting placement. However, a pro-active follow up call may gain more information about placement opportunities, and demonstrate initiative and determination to the organisation – just the qualities they were looking for in the new engineering project team!

Applications – tips from organisations

Every year, we receive numerous CVs and letters with basic spelling mistakes, grammatical errors or sentences that just don't make sense. Nearly all will be discarded straight away. (Financial Services Company)

We consider direct applications – so it is important that applicants research us in advance, and clearly show how they could achieve development with us, as well as giving something to the organisation. (Zurich Financial Services Group)

Checklist

Getting this stage of your placement applications right will require a lot of time. But the more work you put into it, the more likely you are to be successful.

1 Look at the competence examples table, and build up brief notes which you can use in interviews to demonstrate the competences which potential employers are looking for.
2 Practise with a friend, or your placement office, answering competence-based interview questions (more advice on interviews is also given in the next chapter).
3 Prepare a generic CV and a generic enquiry letter – but make sure that you tailor these specifically to the organisation to which you are applying. Ask your placement officer to look at these and comment on them.

Chapter 4

Interviews and Assessment Centres

If you are shortlisted for a placement or internship, you will often be required to attend interviews and an assessment centre. There is a lot you can do to prepare for this, and so improve your chances of success.

4.1 What are assessment centres?

Assessment centres are extensively used for graduate recruitment to many organisations, and increasingly for some or all of the internship/placement process. In many cases, your attendance at an assessment centre will leave you competing against a large number of similar candidates ... and remember, these are from a population which has already been shortlisted. So it is important that you go in as well prepared as possible. This chapter will help in those preparations.

The aim of the assessment centre is to test your capabilities and workplace fit, and so the multiple tests are usually more reliable than one selection test alone. Typically, they will include examples from the following list:

- Pre-assessment web-based screening.

- One or several interviews.

- A short presentation.

- Team or group problem-solving exercises.

- Numerical, spatial and verbal reasoning tests.

- Psychometric tests.

- In-tray exercises.

- (Less often) an essay or report.

Only the most able candidates can perform strongly in all these skills without much preparation. For too many candidates, learning from a series of good and bad experiences is the norm. However, in this chapter we will help you to prepare well in advance, in order to make the best possible use of those assessment centres to which you are invited, and to increase your chances of being able to chose a placement from your preferred list of organisations.

Tips for assessment centres

- Be prepared to move quickly from one assessment session to another.
- Remember that most candidates will be nervous. Do not think you can identify key competitors, and then try to compete with them – there will be other assessment days and as you compete with someone else in the team, these other applicants will be quietly gaining ground out of your sight.
- Keep trying your best in all the sessions – do not let a bad session (for example, a presentation) get you down.
- Remember that you are being observed all the time: let your hair down after you have left the premises, not while you are still there!
- Be punctual – do not be late arriving or for any of your tests and interviews.
- Be well prepared – show your commitment to the organisation, and that you have worked out how and why you could fit into it.

4.2 How to prepare for interviews

Congratulate yourself that you have got this far! But do remember that this is only the start of the process. You now need to make sure that you understand your target placement organisation in more depth than you had prepared for in your original application, and ask yourself how you can contribute to that organisation and for what reasons.

The first place to start is with the organisation's website: understand its size, operations, products and services, and geographical spread. If it has an annual report online, take a look at that: see where it has been successful, and where it may have failed to meet expectations. Read its 'working for us' section as well, and get an idea of how people management may operate in this organisation.

See also if there are wider press articles relevant to that organisation over the past two to three years. Do these tell a different story from the organisation's media sites?

Bearing all of this in mind, ask yourself:

- How might you fit in with this organisation?

- What will you include as your question areas for clarification when you visit the organisation?

- What two to three pithy questions will you ask during your interview?

Web-based or telephone screening

Increasingly, large organisations will use web-based or telephone screening to eliminate those candidates who lack the verbal or numerical reasoning which they require. Sometimes, web-based tests also seek more demanding information on your competences and skills to do a job. So it is very important that you pass the web-based screening assessment.

As with assessment centre tests, your live test is not the place to start practising working with numbers again if you have not done much numeracy work during the previous two to four years. Neither should you begin verbal reasoning tests without prior preparation. Spend some time doing practice tests beforehand, using self-help books available from the larger bookshops (see Further Reading at the end of this chapter). Some tests are also available online, but do ensure that they are of a graduate entry standard. Also, some quality newspapers will include executive tests in their 'careers' or 'work' sections.

Interviews

You may have already had experience of being interviewed for vacation employment, university entry, or for other reasons. Whilst these may have helped you to become familiar with what it feels like to be interviewed, your placement interviews are likely to be very different.

There is no standard format for what you may expect from the way interviews are conducted. These may be done initially on the telephone, face to face with one person,or face to face with several people. You may be in luck, and will be the first (or last) candidate your interviewer sees that day, and so more able to leave a lasting impression. Similarly, you may have an empathetic interviewer, or one who is so aggressive towards you, it leaves you wondering how you were shortlisted in the first place! But whichever style you encounter, remember that you have a key role in whether the interview is successful. Good preparation is essential.

- What have you researched about the organisation, its key objectives, and the issues it is facing?

- How will you articulate your competence and skills, using the Competence Example Table (see Table 3.2)? It is pointless spending time preparing your application and travelling to the interview, but not spending the 15 minutes required to research the organisation you say you want to join.

- Decide now what types of questions you will ask which will demonstrate an intelligent and lively interest in the organisation.

- What will you do to balance the tone of the interview and make the discussion interesting and lively, without using inappropriate humour?

- Make sure that you are appropriately dressed both for your assessments and interviews.

Having reached the interview stage, you will now be competing against similarly qualified people, with a similar drive and potential to your own. Especially in medium and larger organisations, you will usually be interviewed by trained and experienced interviewers who, in some cases, will also be specialised in recruiting and developing graduate trainees and intern/placement students.
   Interviews may be:

- Highly structured, and usually based on competences: for example, 'Give me an example of how you have had to deal with a difficult customer issue, and how you resolved it'. (For other typical questions see the previous chapter and the section on competences.)

- Semi-structured, so questions will be partly based on competences, but will also include follow-up questions: for example, 'You say that you helped resolve a team problem, but what does that tell you about working in groups generally?'

- Unstructured, but these tend to be less commonly used because they make it so difficult to draw fair comparisons between candidates, especially when large numbers of candidates are being interviewed. These interviews are the most difficult to prepare for, but good preparation overall will reduce the chances of you being caught out.

Whichever interview format is used, there are predictable areas you also need to prepare for, as follows:

- 'I've read your CV, but tell me about yourself' – often asked at the beginning. Do not spend too long on your early career, instead reinforce relevant current competences and achievements.

- What makes you different/better from the other candidates?

- Which other placements have you applied for? Why? Which would be your preferred placement?

- What questions do you have for us? (Good questions: 'What do you see as the main priorities in this role over the next 18–24 months?' 'Learning and development are important to me. How would this be supported?' 'Where did the previous job holder go after doing this job?')

- What have been your greatest achievements/disappointments? What are your development areas/weaknesses? Respond positively and show how these have proved to be strengths.

Things to focus on in interviews

Identify and prepare for predictable questions in advance, but don't make your answers sound scripted (see Table 3.2).

Use good eye contact to engage all those people interviewing you.

Present yourself positively, but do not lie or bend the truth: you do not know what the interviewer is seeking, and when you are not candid you will often be found out immediately or later on – and will thereby lose your credibility as a candidate.

Watch your body language and maintain a positive body posture: hands on the table, sit upright.

Listen to the question, and check back if you don't understand it.

You may be asked questions based on when things went wrong: have these prepared – focus on answers where you recovered a situation well.

Have some questions ready for the interviewer(s). Good ones are those which:

- Focus on the organisation's priorities, for example, 'What do you personally see as the key priorities during the next few years, and why?'
- Demonstrate your own desire to learn and develop, for example, 'What could I expect after my initial training here?'
- Show that you have researched the organisation in advance, for example, 'I was interested in the company's problems with product x, and how these were resolved'.
- Gain useful information for you, and show that you can challenge where necessary, for example, 'What was the drop out rate from your graduate recruitment after three years? Why was this?' 'What proportion of your placement students are offered graduate traineeships?'

You may be asked an opening question, to introduce yourself (for example, 'I've read your CV, but tell me a bit about yourself in your own words'), or to summarise why you should be considered for the placement at the end of the interview. Make sure that you have prepared a few sentences beforehand.

What students say they found most challenging in the selection process

- Telephone interviews: here it is difficult to 'read' the interviewer's response to questions, especially for competence-based questions.
- Face-to-face interviews and competence questions.
- Translating what they had written on a CV to show how it could benefit the company.
- Preparing a covering letter with an application.
- Struggling to find (competence) examples which would differentiate them from other candidates.
- How to talk about themselves without sounding too self-obsessed.
- Getting feedback: but to always ask for it and never give up.
- The in-tray exercise! To prioritise time better and look at the overall exercise first, rather than doing each task, one by one.

4.3 How to make a good presentation

You may be asked to do a presentation at your assessment centre. For some centres you will be told about this, and given the presentation topic before the assessment centre day. More usually, you will be told that you will need to do a presentation, but not be told the topic until the assessment centre day itself.

Managing your presentation will help you to avoid presentation disasters

Check *what* you want to say, *how* you will say it, and *what you will use* to say it.

Take control of the environment in which you will be presenting: move the flip chart to where you really want it; make sure that PCs and data projectors are working and decide where you want them.

One nervous candidate had to do a presentation to a group at a global investment bank. Coming through the railway station that morning, she was given a pen. In the presentation, she fiddled with this pen, and then gradually used it as a pointer for her presentation. At the end, participants were asked to give feedback. After a short silence, one delegate said, 'nice pen'. She looked down to see that her free pen was for an exhibition on sex – understandably, it was difficult to continue with a serious discussion after this point.

When you know in advance that you will be doing a presentation

If you are told in advance, then also make sure who will be in the room, what presentation facilities you will have, and the presentation topic.

Check carefully how much time you will have for the presentation and the resources (flip chart, data projector, computer, etc.) that may be available to you, and then prepare your material. Remember the following steps:

1   Who are your audience here? What will they know? What will they need to have explained? What key points do you want to get across?

2   Plan your presentation. It must have a clear structure. A good general structure for any presentation is:

- A personal introduction.

- An explanation of how the presentation will be structured: explain that you will take any questions at the end.

- The aims of the presentation.

- The background relating to the issue.

- The content of your points:

    What (what you are saying and why this matters)

    Why (your rationale)

    How (the resources required, costs, etc.)

    When (timing)

    Risks/constraints

- Conclusions – a short summary of what you have said:

    Issues

    Time

    Cost

    Other

    (No new points introduced here)

- Any questions?

As you prepare the content, think about how the audience will be able to absorb this – good clear points which can be remembered are better than many different points without an overall sense of direction or a conclusion. And once you have planned a presentation, you must rehearse it: your first rehearsal should not be when you actually present it to the organisation! When you feel ready to do so, ask a friend to watch your presentation and give honest feedback. Think about how and when (usually at the end) you will deal with questions and also deal with any resistance to your arguments. Think also about how you will cope if something goes wrong (for example, a projector bulb dying during your presentation) and what contingencies you will need (paper copies to hand out?).

On the day itself:

- Make sure you have all your presentation materials (a memory stick if you are using a data projector, notes, handouts, visual aids, and materials from any personal portfolio which you have prepared – if you have, or are given, marker pens, make sure they work).

- Think back to a previous time when you presented well – remember what you did, and why it went well. Focus on that success and reproduce it again now.

- As you speak, use a clear voice, with a steady pace.

- Avoid turning your back on the audience (for example, if writing on a flip chart, do so from the side of the chart).

- Engage all of your audience by maintaining eye contact with each of them as you speak.

- Use any speaking notes as 'prompts': do not read from scripts.

- However nervous you might be, step outside yourself. Treat the presentation as a rehearsed 'act', or 'mini play'. Do not over-dramatise, but let your enthusiasm and energy come through in what you say and how you say it.

- Keep an eye on the time.

When you don't know in advance that you will have to do a presentation

It is possible that you will arrive at an assessment centre and find out there that you are expected to give a presentation. To prepare for this, you should have a clear idea of what you need as a generic structure, and then use that structure to develop your presentation.

A suitable generic presentation could be like that shown above – try to remember these headings beforehand, or write them on a slip of paper for your wallet or purse, so you can shape your content around these topics.

If you have this overall structure, it should be possible to assemble a clear presentation even at short notice. Keep your presentation notes separate. Bullet points are best. Do not attempt to write a script and then read from it: you probably won't have time, and it is likely to sound wooden.

It also helps to have some visual aids. If you have the time and facilities, use PowerPoint, or alternatively a neatly written set of flip chart pages.

4.4 How to prepare for group exercises

With adequate preparation and practice, applicants will be usually well prepared for interviews, but less ready for other tests at the assessment centre. For many placement (and graduate recruitment) candidates, their individual performance in group work and assessment tests is the make or break factor in whether they are successful with their application. So it is important to understand what organisations are looking for in these exercises, and to maximise your impact.

Brief background on group dynamics

Before we discuss how you should prepare for group exercises, we will look briefly at a model of how groups, and people within groups, behave. First, consider how groups behave. You may have experienced these as quiet and polite in the beginning, noisy later on, and then settling back down to work. Tuckman (1965) observed that groups seemed to go through the following stages as they tackled tasks, as summarised briefly below:

1 Forming: the group works out what it needs to do, and people get to know each other. In this phase, group members may be reserved, polite, and confused.

2 Storming: as the group starts to work, conflicts may develop between group members. Some group members may appear over active, others may appear to withdraw from the discussion.

3 Norming: differences in opinions gradually resolve as group members focus on the required task. Co-operation and shared responsibility develop.

4 Performing: the group develops efficiently and effectively in its task. There is interdependence between group members.

There are no time expectations for how long each of these stages may last. However, if you are aware of these stages, you will be better able to judge how your group is progressing.

What employers are looking for

Most organisations use group work exercises to look for candidates who can contribute well to a group discussion, without dominating it, and can show both independent thinking, and an ability to think and interact with other members of the team to achieve the team goals. However, what sounds simple enough in theory becomes much more challenging when you are competing and observed in unfamiliar surroundings, with unfamiliar people. So it is useful to know what employers are looking for, and to practise these skills in advance.

You will perform well in group exercises if you can:

- *Research your target organisations beforehand.* What are the types of issues which they are coping with, and what opportunities are they developing? What does the business press say about them? What types of topics might they raise in group discussions (but do not expect that you will be able to guess the topic beforehand)? What have interns and placement students found out about the organisation from previous placements? Who are their main competitors and what do they offer that the application organisation does not offer?

- *Understand what the exercise requires.* Think about what you need to work through in this exercise. Many tasks will have similar underlying themes, so have a checklist of what needs to be done:

    The task.

    The resources available and their limitations (money, time, physical resources, knowledge, etc.).

    Who are the key stakeholders directly and indirectly affected by the task? How will they be managed?

    What are the key risk factors in completing, or failing to complete the task? How should they be managed?

- *Speak effectively.* Plan to speak at least four or five times during the discussion. Have a sense of what you will say, but remember that you need to listen to others too, so you may need to adapt what you say. As you speak, engage all those around the table with eye contact.

- *Listen effectively.* We work in teams to share knowledge and understanding, and to come up with better solutions than if we worked alone. So good listening is key: what has the other person said, how does it fit with, and modify, your own thinking? As well as listening effectively, you can often help the group to develop its effectiveness by reinforcing and developing another team member's point. For example, 'I liked Sophie's ideas about … and I feel we could develop these further if we … '. As you develop these techniques, you are helping the group to progress and develop its achievement towards the task, and may make some allies along the way too!

- *Use your thinking ability.* The exercise may be designed around a theme with which nobody is likely to be familiar, or, more likely, one where each group member is likely to know something which would help to solve the group task. So, as you read the exercise brief, analyse those areas where you do have knowledge/thoughts so you can make a contribution, and think also about those areas where you may not have knowledge.

    Is there an analytical model that you have used in your studies which can help you, and other members of the group in this task?

    Use creative thinking where appropriate.

Help the group get unstuck, when it loses momentum. Use incisive questions to cut through the assumptions which may be holding the group back. For example, 'Why does this make a difference?'

Is the task similar to something you have previously encountered? What are those similarities? And the critical differences?

- *Involve all the team members.* In some teams, those team members with some of the best ideas, thinking and insights will remain silent. So, if there are team members who remain quiet, and you have already established your own place and voice in the team, get some of the quieter members involved too, with phrases such as, 'I'd be interested in Mark's ideas on this project …'.

- *Keep track of the time.* There are many reasons why groups will fail to complete an exercise: sometimes they are designed that way, or the end result is of less importance to recruiters than the process of the group and the skills demonstrated by group candidates. Most often, however, groups simply become so engrossed in the task that they lose all track of time. Remember to do this yourself and thus pick up some easy ticks on the assessors' checklists: tell the group when you are half way through the allotted time, tell the group when you are three quarters through the allotted time, and finally when you have five minutes left. As you give these time checks, try also to give a realistic summary of the group's progress, and an upbeat message about the need to continue to focus in order to get the task successfully completed.

- *Ensure that the group remains focused on the task.* But do not end up as the group's policeman! If you find that people are drifting off the subject, use phrases such as 'OK, we have a task to complete here, and we need to refocus on it', or 'OK, let's get back to the task. How are we doing?'.

Things to avoid in group exercises

Saying nothing!
Saying too much and/or too loudly.
Repeating what someone else has already said.
Interjecting 'I was just going to say that … '.
Speaking to only one or two people in the group: as you speak, establish eye contact with everyone in the group.
Speaking to your shoes.
Inappropriately attacking another person's point of view.
Using inappropriate humour.
Showing arrogance towards other team members.

How you can get ready for group exercises

1   Practise! Good practice is key to improved group performance. If several of you are seeking placements and internships, spend some time doing practice sessions. Use one or two of the group as observers, together with 'What employers are looking for' section above, as a checklist to give feedback.

   Ask your university placement team if they will help the group run some practice group working exercises, or arrange these for yourselves.

   In tutorial sessions, get used to speaking to small groups by volunteering to present to the tutorial group whenever you can. Seek constructive feedback from your fellow students and your tutor about your presentation style.

2   Practise active listening. In your practice groups, set a rule: each speaker must make three contributions to the discussion, but before speaking, they must repeat the final sentence of the previous speaker. This will show you how difficult it can be to prepare your own contribution to the group, while at the same time, really listening to what your colleagues are saying!

4.5 Tests and other exercises

You may be required to undertake tests, such as psychometric or personality tests, verbal, numerical and spatial reasoning tests. A few organisations may use other tests than these, such as in-tray exercises and wider knowledge tests. Many of these are also done 'online', and may be used as part of an early pre-selection and shortlisting.

Psychometric tests

Organisations may ask you to undertake a variety of psychometric tests in order to get a better understanding of your personality – the kind of person you are (personality tests), and your understanding of numbers, words and abstract reasoning (ability).

   Personality tests which you might typically encounter are:

1   The Myers-Briggs Personality Test

   You will be given a bank of questions to answer, and from this your tendency to be one of the following personality types will be assessed:

   Extravert or Introvert

   Sensing or Intuition

   Thinking or Feeling

   Judging or Perceiving

2   Cattell's 16 PF personality questionnaire

Again, you will be given a bank of questions to answer, and from this, the organisation will be able to judge on personality traits such as: warmth; reasoning; emotional stability; dominance; liveliness; rule consciousness; social boldness; sensitivity; vigilance; abstractedness; privateness; apprehension; openness to change; self-reliance; perfectionism; tension.

In each case, these descriptions of personality types have special meanings, which may not be the same as day-to-day colloquial usage (for example, in the Myers-Briggs, intuition means that the person showing this trait is more likely to trust information which is abstract and theoretical, and to be interested in future possibilities, rather than the opposite type (sensing) who is more likely to be interested in detail and factual information).

Organisations using these types of tests will have a variety of motivations for doing so. Most often, personality tests may be used to identify factors which will be explored further during interviews if you score especially high or low in a particular personality attribute.

It is difficult and unwise to try to second guess what is required, and so 'massage' your answers. However, if you believe that psychometric tests will be used in an assessment centre you will be attending, one way in which you can prepare is to do the tests in advance, and consider how you might respond in interview to questions about particularly high or low scores in any of the tested areas.

Despite their widespread use and misuse in selection decisions, personality testing remains controversial. It assumes that an accurate assessment can and has been made about what a job requires (rather than a general impression review), and that personality test results can predict future success (it is debatable whether they can predict job success, let alone career success). In most cases, it is unlikely that a decision to engage or reject you would be based on personality tests in this factor alone. But if you are repeatedly rejected on the basis of your psychometric test results, you may be trying to enter a role which is not suitable for you, so it is important, once again, that you ask for detailed feedback from those organisations which reject you for a placement.

Ability tests – verbal, numerical and abstract reasoning tests

These are designed to check your overall ability, and will usually measure you against a known population of graduates or undergraduates. Even if you had been good in these areas earlier in your studies, a lack of recent practice may make you slower in test conditions or lagging behind in technique. So, unlike personality tests, you can probably improve your test scores if you practise these types of tests beforehand. Test books are available in the larger bookshops, and a selection of titles is shown at the end of this chapter. If your answers are weak when you first do the practice tests, look behind what the question was about. Over time your scores should improve and may get you in the right mindset to maximise your score when you are in the assessment centre.

In-tray exercises and wider knowledge tests

These are less widely used these days, but it is still possible that you could encounter them. An in-tray exercise gives you a variety of situations – some trivial, others critical – to consider, and then decide how you will proceed with them. You will do this on a timed basis. Be clear about your overall objectives and priorities, then go through the in-tray accordingly. Before you start in detail, quickly scan the whole of the in-tray, and prioritise those items which are most important and require your attention first. As with exams, watch your time and answer with reasonable quality as many problems as you can – do not go into excessive detail on only one or two topics.

Special skills and aptitudes

If you claim to have a special skill (languages, professional knowledge, IT skills, etc.), you may be asked to demonstrate this when you visit the organisation: so make sure that you describe such skills appropriately in your application! Similarly, if you are interviewed for a specialist area, you may be asked questions that are specific to that specialisation. For example, if you are applying for a role in engineering, languages, marketing, PR, or advertising, make sure that you have two or three examples which you can discuss with authority and interest. As you do so, you will demonstrate your initiative in having undertaken this background work.

> ### Where students fail in assessment centres: organisations' views
>
> A lack or very limited understanding of the organisation and its history.
> No understanding/enthusiasm of the role for which they have applied.
> An inability to give competence examples in interviews.
> A lack of commercial awareness/interest.
> Poor interpersonal skills fit.
> Poor group/teamwork.
> Arrogance – appearing to expect a job as a matter of right.
> A lack of personal drive and commitment.
> An overall poor interview performance.
> A failure to get feedback from recruiters on unsuccessful assessments, and to learn from previous mistakes.

Where students fail in selection procedures: university views

Many universities will provide advice and practice sessions in CVs, interviews, assessment centres, and psychometric tests for placement and graduate recruitment. Despite this, they report that some students often have the following difficulties:

They dislike telephone interviews.
They lack a readiness for psychometric tests.
They have trouble with online application forms (content and time taken to complete).
They lack confidence/have over confidence in their own skills and abilities.
They lack an understanding of the roles for which they are applying.
They fail to tailor applications to specific or role opportunities.
Some lack commercial awareness.
They need to refine their interview skills.
They show arrogance and give organisations the impression 'you are lucky to have found me'.

4.6 Seeking and getting feedback on how you have done

Whether you are successful or unsuccessful in your assessment centre, always ask for specific and individual feedback on how you did. It is not enough to know 'there were many good candidates', or 'you were obviously not having a good day' ... nor is it enough to take the easy option and not ask for any feedback. You need to know how you did in each of the tests: the strengths you demonstrated and where you needed to be more effective. Write down this feedback, and use the information you have gained to develop your performance next time round.

If you were unsuccessful, then after you have received your feedback think about how you will use it to be more effective next time. Console yourself with the knowledge that any assessment process has a high level of subjectivity – even assessment centres, which are normally regarded as the most reliable approach to selection, have a predictive accuracy of about 60–65 per cent. So the right organisation is out there, waiting for you to find them and impress them. If you did give your best at that organisation and still were unsuccessful, then maybe it was not the right one for you, and you will almost certainly be better off elsewhere.

And if you were successful with your assessment centre, well done! Now you can apply the same level of method and determination outlined in this book to make the most of your organisational experience.

4.7 Summary

Good preparation for assessment centres is time consuming but essential. Remember, with many candidates arriving at assessment centres under-prepared, such good preparation on your part will put you into a stronger competitive position.

Prepare each element of your assessment centre thoroughly. Do not expect to succeed by ad-libbing on the day.

Your university is a great source of support for interviews and assessments, so do ask them for help.

You will be successful, but may suffer rejections on the way – try to learn from these experiences.

4.8 Further reading

Barrett, J. (2004) *Aptitude, Personality and Motivation Tests*. London: Kogan Page.

Bright, J. and Earl, J. (2007) *Brilliant CVs* (3rd edn). Harlow: Pearson.

Byron, M. (2002) *How to Pass Advanced Numeracy Tests*. London: Kogan Page.

Hodgson, S. (2007) *Brilliant Answers to Tough Interview Questions* (3rd edn). London: Pearson, Prentice Hall.

Kline, N. (1999) *Time to Think*. London: Cassell Illustrated.

Kourdi, J. (2008) *Succeed at Psychometric testing – Verbal Reasoning Advanced Level*. London: Hodder Arnold.

Perkins, G. (2007) *Killer CVs and Hidden Approaches* (3rd edn). Harlow: Pearson.

Weissman, J. (2008) *Presenting to Win*. Harlow: FT/Prentice Hall.

Williams, L. (2008) *Readymade CVs*. London: Kogan Page.

Checklist

1 Practise numeracy and verbal reasoning tests. If you can't afford to buy practice books for verbal and numerical, and abstract reasoning, share the cost and use of these books with other friends who are preparing for selections.

2 Critically self-review your presentation skills – get extra practice if you need it (seminars, with friends, etc.). Keep a short note on presentation structure in your wallet/purse.

3 Critically self-review your group working and team working skills. How well do you understand how groups work? How effective are you at making your voice heard? How effective are you at listening to others? How effective are you at keeping the group focused on its task, and time keeping?

4 Make sure that you have appropriate clothing, clean and well presented, for your interviews.

5 Before your interview: make sure you have re-read your competence examples table (Chapter 3); make sure that you know what you will say if you are asked to introduce yourself, or to summarise your suitability; identify three or four questions which you will ask at the end of the interview.

6 Ensure that you ask for feedback after your assessment – get details, not generalisations – to understand where you have shown strengths, but make sure also that you know how and why you have underperformed in any area. Write down this feedback, review it as you prepare for your next assessment centre, and understand how you will address any perceived weaknesses.

Chapter 5

The Important
Not-so-Small Print

Chapter contents

As with other aspects of your placement, making sure that you have the basics right in advance will save hassle during, and in many cases after, the placement. The information in this chapter was correct as at December 2008. If you require more up to date information, please see the relevant contact points at the end of this chapter.

5.1 Pay

Not all placements and internships are paid. If, however, you are doing a placement for a period of less than 12 months, and the placement is part of a university course (or the European Union's Leonardo da Vinci or Youth in Action programmes) then employers are *not* required to pay you the national minimum wage if your placement is based in the UK. If however, you are being paid *and* the placement is *not* part of a university placement requirement, then you should receive at least the national minimum wage.

Unpaid placement or internships do exist, but in most cases are only worth considering if they are both short term (days or weeks), and in highly competitive roles where your aim is to have a taste of working in that type of role, and want to develop network contacts for future job applications. Unpaid placements are not suitable if the work is part of your degree course, and if the duration of the placement is likely to last for any substantial period.

So how much can you expect to be paid on your placement? Unfortunately, it is impossible to give any clear advice about this, since it will depend greatly on what your placement is, and where you will be working. For placements which are not part of a university course, the national minimum wage means that you would be paid at least £5.73 per hour if you are aged 22 or over, or the development rate of £4.77 an hour if you are aged 18–21 (rates correct as at 1 October 2008, see http://www. direct.gov.uk/en/Employment/Employees/Pay/ for up to date rates). Despite the lack of legal requirements on employers, for 2008–2009, placement students typically received more than these basic legal minimum rates, and pay was based on an annual salary of £14, 000 and above in many cases.

Remember, however, that whilst pay is important and a welcome relief from living on a student budget, the value of what you are doing and where you are doing your placement is more important for your long-term development. So avoid being exploited by an unscrupulous organisation, but also avoid any unnecessary competition with other placement students about pay levels in this important development year out.

5.2 Managing your personal budget

It is not surprising that most students report that their financial situation improved, or did not get much worse, during their placement year. Few students are able to finish their placements with all their money problems resolved, and some will have unpleasant surprises about unexpected additional costs (for example, suitable clothing for work, travel to/from work, different social patterns where they tended to spend more, and even the higher costs of daily food and drinks). This is especially important if your placement is based in a large city. So, before accepting that dream placement, and a good salary in a glitzy city, do work out your budget carefully and realistically beforehand. Online budgeting tools are available and two examples are included in the Further information section at the end of this chapter.

5.3 Tax

At this stage of your life, paying your tax should not be complicated, but you will need to be organised. Your tax liability depends on your income, *not* on your status as a student. So it is important that you recognise that tax rules may appear different from those if you only worked during your holidays as a student, when you may have signed a form – a P38(S) – because you had not expected to earn as much as the income tax personal allowance threshold.

As a result your pay from the placement will be subject to income tax and national insurance deductions. However, you will not pay tax on the first proportion of your pay (the Personal Allowance, which is £6,475 for the tax year of April 2009 to April 2010). Your tax will be paid on a sliding scale through automatic deductions via your employer, using Pay As You Earn (PAYE).

You will need a current tax code, so that your placement organisation can apply PAYE tax at the correct rate. If you do not have this, you may be charged tax on an emergency tax code basis, which will mean that you will pay tax at a much higher rate than you need to. If this happens, you will usually be able to claim a tax refund, but your cash flow will obviously be affected in the meantime.

To ensure that you are paying the correct tax, you should:

1   Contact the Inland Revenue (http://www.hmrc.gov.uk/index.htm) for a tax code, if you do not have one already.

2   If you are already working, for example in a part-time job, ensure that you obtain a P45 tax form from your employer as you leave – usually this will be sent to you automatically, but make sure you have it before you start your placement. Take your P45 from your previous employment to your placement organisation on the first day, or as soon as reasonably practical after this.

3   Check your tax code on your first salary pay slip. In particular, if it shows BR, you may be paying too much tax, so you should immediately contact the tax office to get your correct code.

5.4 Tax credits

If you are responsible for the care of a child, you may be eligible for a Child Tax Credit or Working Tax Credit. If you are already receiving either form of credit, remember that as you start and finish your placement this will affect your level of income and so your eligibility for Working Tax Credits and Child Tax Credits, so do remember to notify the Tax Credit Helpline to avoid an under or over payment of credits. Some organisations give help with childcare or offer childcare vouchers, and this may also affect your level of tax credit to which you might be entitled. For further details, see http://www.hmrc.gov.uk/taxcredits/

5.5 National insurance

If you earn more than £110 a week (April 2009–April 2010 tax year), you will need to pay National Insurance on your pay during your placement.

The rates payable will vary according to pension arrangements in your placement organisation, and will contribute in the longer term to your own state pension contributions.

When you start your placement, your employer will need your national insurance number. If you are a UK citizen, this will have been sent to you automatically when you were younger; it will also be shown on your P45 tax form.

Visitors to the UK from overseas will not have received a National Insurance number automatically. If this applies to you, and you do not already have a National Insurance number for casual employment whilst a student, you should apply for one as soon as possible. Obtaining a National Insurance number usually takes a few weeks. You will be required to attend an interview, and will need to show documentary evidence about your identity and status before the national insurance number is issued to you. For further information, see http://www.dwp.gov.uk/lifeevent/benefits/ ni_number. asp#where

5.6 Right to work in the UK as an international student

To comply with UK law (Immigration and Asylum Act 1996) your employer will ask you to prove that you have the right to work in the UK.

If you are a British citizen, or a citizen from a country within the European Economic Area (EEA) or Switzerland, you will have the right to work in the UK. However, employers are required by law to verify this right, and this is most often done by asking to see, and taking a copy of, your passport.

Different arrangements apply if you are from countries outside this area. If you are from one of the new European Union accession states (Poland, Lithuania, Estonia, Latvia, Slovenia, Slovakia, Hungary, or the Czech Republic), you may need to register for work under the Worker Registration Scheme, but you will not need to register if you are from Cyprus or Malta. Additional restrictions may also apply if you are from Bulgaria or Romania. (For details of the Worker Registration Scheme, go to http://www.ukba.homeoffice.gov.uk/workingintheuk/eea/wrs/)

If you are from any other country, you should check the visa stamp on your passport. If you have leave to remain in the UK as a student, you may work in the UK, provided that:

- You do not work for more than 20 hours a week, unless the employment is part of your studies or is an internship.

- You do not engage in business, you are not self-employed, or you do not provide services as a professional sportsperson or as an entertainer.

- You do not take a full-time position.

If you do not automatically have the right to work in the UK, but you wish to extend your stay at the end of your course, you may be able to do so for a limited period. For further information please see http://www.ukba.home office.gov.uk/studyingintheuk/extending/

As an overseas student doing your placement in the UK, you will still need to pay UK tax and national insurance deductions from your pay. However, you may be able to reclaim some tax payments when you return home, and you should ask the Tax Office for Form P85.

5.7 Working abroad

Your placement may give you the opportunity to work abroad. Many current and former students working abroad describe it as amongst the most formative and exciting times of their lives. But without dampening your enthusiasm for this, we consider here the practicalities rather than the undoubted opportunities that this would present.

If you are a UK national or a national of a European Economic Area (EEA) or European Union (EU) country, you have the right to work in any other European member state, without the need for a work permit. You will also have the same rights as nationals of your destination country in working conditions, pay and social security matters. If you plan to go outside Europe, your status as a student will often mean that you can apply for special short-term employment visas to cover your placement. However, you cannot take this for granted and should check well in advance of your planned trip, both to confirm your eligibility, and to give you time to seek alternative placement arrangements if this is not possible.

Here are some of the practicalities:

- *Change of culture*: not only will you be changing from 'student' to 'worker', but you will also have different national and different national work cultures to which you must adjust. This is part of the learning process, but may even affect the management style of those supervising your placement.

- *Terms and conditions of employment*: remember that these will also differ from country to country.

- *Social security and health*: within the European Economic Area (EEA) or European Union (EU), you will continue to have protection under European treaties. To qualify for free or reduced cost health care in these areas, ensure that you obtain a European Health Insurance Card before you travel (see http://www.nhs.uk/healthcareabroad/Pages/Healthcareabroad.aspx). Elsewhere, it makes sense to check arrangements before you travel, and you may require additional private insurance protection to cover for this.

- *Budgets in a different country*: the cost of living can vary considerably from country to country, and different tax rates may mean that the pay you think you will receive gives you more, or less, purchasing power than you were expecting. Get as much information as you can in advance about this.

- *Safety and security*: For current information about security in your host country, see the UK Foreign and Commonwealth Office website (http://www.fco. gov.uk/en/travelling-and-living-overseas/travel-advice-by-country/).

- *UK tax*: If you normally live and study in the UK, but your placement is overseas during the year, then your overseas pay will still be liable for UK tax. However, if you also pay tax on your overseas earnings, you should be able to claim a deduction from your UK tax liability when you return to the UK. If you have worked overseas during your placement, and paid tax in your host country, don't forget to enquire whether you can apply for a tax refund when you return to the UK.

5.8 Keeping track of your employment record

It may seem obvious, but it is essential to keep track of your own employment record, especially if you are working abroad. One student commented

> I had no idea that my work overseas would have caused so many problems when I finally graduated. I applied to do teaching, and although I successfully got a job, my references check delayed the start of my job for over two months, as they checked my overseas employment record.

As you progress, make sure that you keep the names and contact details of two or three people who will be able to provide a reference on your behalf when you finally graduate – this is especially important if you work abroad. In all cases, you must keep a record of where you have worked, and the dates when you did so. Some employers will check every job you have done, anywhere in the world. The list of jobs requiring detailed employment checks is longer than you might think, and includes teaching and roles where you may come into contact with children or vulnerable adults, jobs in the financial services, and many roles in the public sector or for registration with professional bodies.

5.9 Safety at work

Your personal health, safety, and security are very important, and so is the safety of your colleagues, and those visiting your place of work.

Your placement organisation has a statutory duty to provide you with a safe place to work, under the terms of the Health and Safety at Work Act 1974, and subsequent regulations. But the duty to provide a safe place of working rests with the individual employee too. The law requires individual employees to:

- Take reasonable care for the health and safety of themselves and others who may be adversely affected by their acts or omissions at work.

- Co-operate with their employer as is necessary to enable health and safety requirements to be met (Health and Safety at Work Act 1974, Section 7).

In addition, employees have a duty to:

- Use any protective equipment which is provided; to ensure that it is correctly stored, and to report any loss or obvious defect.

- Ensure that laid-down systems of work are followed, for example during manual handling operations.

- Tell their employer of any serious or immediate dangers in health and safety.

It is therefore important that you pay attention to your own health and safety, and that of your colleagues. In practice, this may mean:

- Making sure that you attend, and pay full attention to, health and safety training which is offered by your employer – this will include fire and security precautions, and may also include safe lifting and handling aggression from service users.

- If you are asked to do any form of risk assessment, you must do so diligently and carefully.

5.10 Help with terms and conditions of employment in the UK

For the vast majority of placement students, their placement will prove to be an enjoyable and rewarding experience. However, whilst you are on your placement, if you are experiencing difficulties with the terms of your employment, you should speak first to your manager. If this does not resolve the issue, speak to your Placement Office for further advice. If you are a member of a trade union, your trade union officer may also be able to help.

However, there are also free and confidential helplines available to you, including:

The Advisory Conciliation and Arbitration Service (ACAS)
The Labour Relations Agency (LRA) if you are in Northern Ireland
The Citizen's Advice Bureau (CAB)

5.11 Further information

Tax information
http://www.hmrc.gov.uk/index.htm

National minimum wage
The National Minimum Wage is usually reviewed annually in October.
For information on current levels, see http://www.direct.gov.uk/en/
Employment/Employees/Pay/DG_10027201

Tax credits (if you have children)

http://www.taxcredits.inlandrevenue.gov.uk/Qualify/WhatAreTax.Credits.
aspx

Managing money
For an excellent and independent site to help you plan your money, see
http://www.whataboutmoney.info/student_money/england/. This includes
a budget format developed by UCAS for students, and a tax link to help
calculate your own tax and estimate whether you have under/over paid.
For a very easy to use, alternative online budget calculator, see also the
Financial Services Authority guide http://www.moneymadeclear.fsa.gov.
uk/tools.aspx?Tool=budget_calculator

Right to work in the UK
To check your eligibility to work in the UK, go to
http://ukba.homeoffice.gov.uk/workingintheuk/

Working abroad
For general employment advice, see
http://www.direct.gov.uk/en/BritonsLivingAbroad/EducationAndJobs/
DG_4014676
For information about safety and security, see http://www.fco.gov.uk/en/
travelling-and-living-overseas/travel-advice-by-country/
Remember, you will also need to think about employment regulations
in your host country, and you will need to research this separately.

Checklist

1 Make sure that your tax code is up to date.
2 If you are a visitor to the UK, ensure that you have a National
   Insurance Number.
3 Work out your new personal budget for your placement.
4 Remember to keep a note of two or three people who would give
   you a reference from each organisation you work for – keep full
   contact details of these referees for when you graduate.

5 Keep track of your employment start and finish dates.
6 Tax can become messy if you don't start off correctly: make sure you have a tax code and your P45, and this will get things straight from the outset.
7 If you have a child, check your eligibility for tax credits.
8 Planning to work abroad? Plan carefully. Start by checking early on that you have the right to visit the country of your choice and to be paid for your placement. Think also about your budget whilst living abroad.
9 When you start work, treat matters of health, safety, and security seriously – you are legally required to do so, and have a duty to look after yourself and others you are in contact with at work.

Section 2

Managing Your Placement

Your placement is a fantastic opportunity to live, feel and breathe how organisations really work, so make the most of it. Aside from your university assignments (which we cover separately in Chapter 9), the three key areas to focus on in your placement are:

1 Settling into your role – dealing with the day-to-day issues, and being aware of your rights and responsibilities in the workplace (Chapter 6).

2 Being effective in work – your next priority is to become effective in the workplace as soon as possible, and to operate effectively in activities which you may have not had much involvement in previously. You may have already studied these, but in Chapter 7, we give you practical advice and guidance on key skills to help you become more effective, more quickly, in the workplace.

3 Being effective in learning and development – you will need to show that you are learning for your university, and your organisation will certainly want to see that you are developing your competences and skills effectively. If you are also preparing for professional exams, you may need to show that you are working up your Continued Professional Development (CPD) too. With good personal organization, you should be able to cover all these angles. In Chapter 8, we take you through the key steps in this to make the most of your learning during your placement.

Chapter 6

Settling into Your Placement

Chapter contents

Made it! But how do you make the most of it? As well as missing family and friends, perhaps living in a new place, the student now has to balance this with working well in the placement organisation(s). This is a good time to think in more detail about what you want to get from your placement, and how you will judge whether or not it has been successful. You will have some key goals, but start to think outside the obvious, and make a note of these goals in your learning journal (Chapter 8). As an example, here is a selection of comments on how students have judged whether or not their placement has been successful:

How will you judge success? Student views

Being offered a job at the end.
Winning sales/service competitions.
Real sense of self-achievement.
Knowing I was learning the work.
Understanding what I want to do/do not want to do in the future.

(Cont'd)

Feeling part of a motivated and challenging department.
Understanding how a business really works.
The contribution I made through my project.
Somewhere I could picture myself working in the future; feeling I fit in.
Gaining extra work-based qualifications (e.g. project management).
Doing practical things (sales, conference organisation, marketing, pro-grammes, writing machine code used across the organisation, etc.).
Responsibility in people management.

6.1 Settling into your new workplace: what you can expect, what to sort out for yourself

When you start work, you will need to take your:

- Tax P45 form from previous employment; if this is your first job, you will need your National Insurance number.

- Your bank details, for payment of your salary.

- Proof that you are eligible to work in the UK, usually your passport.

- You may also need to take in your relevant education certificates.

When you receive your pay slip, check that you have been given a tax code (numbers followed by a letter). If your tax code is shown as only two letters, you are likely to be paying too much tax, so you must contact the tax office to be allocated a correct tax code (HM Revenue and Customs). You may be eligible for a tax refund, so do keep your pay slips in a safe place; and when you leave the placement, keep your new P45 tax summary safe as well.

Check what other benefits your employer may have available, such as season ticket loans, sports and social facilities, etc. And while it might seem a long time in the future, think about whether you can set aside a small proportion of your salary for a pension fund. The earlier you can affordably start to do this the better, but do make sure you take advice before making any commitments.

6.2 Workplace etiquette

There will be various forms of workplace etiquette which you will need to observe. These may be formally stated (for example, in the organisation's policies and rules), or not formally stated, because 'everybody knows them' – except, perhaps, the new placement student. So find out what is acceptable and not acceptable. This may include such apparently trivial things as the accepted dress code, preferred times for lunch breaks, and so on. As a placement student, colleagues will tend to be more forgiving as you settle into the workplace, but they will also expect you to be committed, interested, and conscientious.

6.3 In-company assessments: performance management and talent reviews

During your first two to three weeks, make sure that you find out how your host organisation will judge your work success. This may be covered in your induction process, but even if it is not, ask your line manager.

Whichever approach your host organisation uses to assess your performance, it is essential that you:

- Find out what the process is.

- Understand what your assessment criteria will be.

- Take ownership of the process and actively manage yourself.

What processes might organisations use?

Some organisations will include you in their standard performance management review process. Your line manager will discuss specific work objectives with you, and tell you the intervals when these objectives and goals will be discussed with you, and you will receive formal, written feedback on your progress and work achievements. Typically, these meetings will be every three or six months. Some organisations, however, will review your progress on a monthly basis.

Other organisations will have specific assessment arrangements for their internships. For example, BP use a competence assessment form, where you will be asked to show how your competences are developing. The BP competence framework (see Figure 6.1) also helps you to understand the competences which organisations like BP look for in their university placements. They will consider your work performance, but they will also look more widely at how your competences are developing, and will ask you to undertake a self-assessment of your progress, and to present this to your manager.

But not all organisations have formal organisation assessment processes for their students. For example, in the UK Border Agency, students are given regular feedback on their contributions to team activities, and this forms the basis of feedback to their university. Even if no formal assessment criteria are used by your placement organisation, you will help your own learning and development if you use one of the competence frameworks shown in this book to track and record your own

Competency Assessment	Student Name:	
Competencies	Behavioural Definition	Evidence
Technical Understanding • Knowledge of fundamentals and application ability • Familiarity with computer tools • Motivation and ability to learn • Comprehension of complex tasks • Relevance of academic pursuit, specialised skills, and previous work experiences		
Thinking • Situation and problem definition • Identifies key issues in a complex situation • Draws logical conclusions/anticipates consequences • Sees the merits of differing positions or opposing viewpoints • Willing to challenge traditional thinking • Innovation in adapting ideas to problems • Sees connections or patterns in seemingly unconnected facts or events	Analytical Thinking – The ability to break down a problem or situation into its component parts, identifying implications and causal relationships. The application of logic. Conceptual Thinking – Recognising patterns and the key underlying issues. Making the complex simple. Finding creative solutions to problems.	
Drive • Plans and organises to complete projects on time • Sets and achieves challenging goals and targets • Digs beneath the obvious to get at the facts • Does things before being asked to or forced to by events • Adapts easily to changes. Adopts multiple roles to meet the situation • Takes steps to overcome obstacles	Proactivity – Taking the initiative. Doing things before being asked or forced by events. Persistent in overcoming obstacles. Going beyond the job description and looking to the future. Spotting and seizing opportunities. Results Orientation – A concern for achieving results. Setting challenging goals. Doing things better, faster, more effectively. Staying focused on goals.	
Influence • Uses information to persuade others to support a position. Explains complex ideas by using well chosen examples • Tailors influencing tactics and language to the audience • Seeks/assumes positions of leadership • Representation of others' interests • Develops team spirit – brings people together. Works to resolve conflicts and differences within the group • Encouragement of others' participation and contribution	Persuasiveness – The ability to convince others of a view, conclusion, position, etc. Getting others to go along with or support one's agenda. Leadership – The ability to develop teamwork and co-operation while leading a group of people, articulating a purpose for the group, and motivating people to fulfil that purpose.	

Competencies	Behavioural Definition	Evidence
Working Together • Makes conscious effort to build rapport with others • Willingness to share information and problem solving • Can understand situation from another's point of view • Demonstrates a willingness to learn from others • Forms alliances/teams/groups to achieve mutually beneficial goals • Listens responsively – is easy to talk to • Coaching and networking ability	Seeing things from another person's point of view. Can understand the perspectives, feelings, and concerns of others and build or maintain relationships with people. The willingness and ability to work co-operatively with others.	
Business/Commercial Sense • Has a clear view of the overall purpose/objectives of the organization • Understands how the project relates to the organisational goals • Works to raise/save/make money • Acts to improve customer satisfaction, productivity, or profitability • Constructs arguments based on economic principles	The tendency to view activities as a means to an end rather than ends in themselves. It includes the desire to make or save money.	

Figure 6.1   **BP competences format (reproduced with permission)**

competences. Utilise these to discuss your progress with your manager, or with your mentor. If this is not possible, try to still use a competence framework to record your progress, and integrate the results with your learning journal.

Formal assessment

Organisations will usually include you in their performance review process, although they may have many different names for this – for example, staff appraisal, performance review, performance development review, etc. But whatever it is called the review will be between you and your line manager on:

• What you need to do (your objectives).

• What you should learn (your learning plan).

• How well you did (performance review).

• What you have learned (learning review).

Work-based objectives

These may be expressed as 'hard measures' (those which can easily be defined by numbers, for example, identifying sales leads, accuracy/error rates, or income goals, delivering work by a specific date), or 'soft measures' (those which cannot easily be described by numbers, for example, how well you fit in with colleagues and the wider team, the perceived quality of your work, etc.).

Your objectives may be described as SMART: Specific goals, Measurable, Achievable, Realistic, and Timed. This will help you and your manager to be clear about what is expected, and so make your performance review more objective. Once SMART objectives have been proposed to you, step back and take a reality check before you agree to them:

- Do you understand what is required?

- Are the goals ambiguous in any way?

- To what extent do you depend on other people before you deliver your objectives?

- Do you have the skills and knowledge to deliver those objectives?

If in any doubt, speak to your manager.

Work-based objectives may be expressed simply as a list of objectives which you are expected to achieve. However, many organisations now structure objectives within a Balanced Scorecard (Kaplan and Norton, 1992). Rather than seeing objectives as a list of objectives, the Balanced Scorecard recognises that a successful organisation can have its major objectives expressed within overall and interconnected headings of:

Learning and Growth > Internal Processes > Customer Perspective > Financial Perspective

The idea of the Balanced Scorecard is that once the organisational scorecard is decided upon, each function/team can develop a scorecard based on its own contribution to delivering the organisation scorecard and the overall strategy. Furthermore, each employee in the organisation should then have an individual Balanced Scorecard, with individual objectives under each of these headings that align with the overall organisational objectives.

Assessment processes

During your placement, you will almost certainly be subject to some forms of assessment, whether by the university, or by your placement organisation manager.

There are two possible types of assessment: performance review (how well you delivered against work plans and objectives) and development reviews (how your learning and development are progressing, against a defined set of competences). Very often the two assessments may be merged together into one review, with evidence from your performance review used to inform your development review.

It is very important that you spend time preparing for these assessments. Within that preparation, you should consider

- What were you required to achieve?

- What SMART information do you have to demonstrate progress and achievement?

- What support/training was required?

- What support/training did you provide to others?

- What level of 'stretch' did your goals require? How much of this was planned? How much was unexpected? Why?

- Were you required to undertake other responsibilities in this time?

- What went well? What went not so well? What learning was achieved? What do you still need by way of learning?

Project team role and performance

You may find that you have a manager who has overall responsibility for you, but that your placement involves working for a variety of project teams. This will mean that your assessment will be based on report(s) from your project team leader(s) during your placement. It will provide excellent experience for you of project team work, which is frequently used by organisations to put work teams together.

Working within a project team usually means that you will be working on a specific deliverable, and often liaising with people across the organisation. You will usually have a clearly defined role, with clearly definable objectives. However, project teams may not always work closely with each other, and projects themselves can be complex and, at times, politically charged work environments. So here it is even more important that you are clear about your work objectives and requirements, and that you do what is required. In Chapter 7, we give an overview of what projects are, and what to look out for if you are on a project team.

Informal assessment

Assessment may not always be formal, and can often include an element of a day-to-day informal assessment of progress. Where you do not know how you are being assessed, people will make judgements based on team or organisational culture … just how well you 'fit' into the organisation. Informal assessment is difficult, and, you may feel, unfair, because it is not transparent. Nevertheless, it is an organisational reality.

Take some time to observe and listen to managers' expectations, and observe how other colleagues appear to be informally assessed. If you are replacing another placement student, discuss the organisation climate, but remember also that personalities change, and that your new colleague may not respond to you in the same way. When you feel you have a reasonable understanding of the informal assessment criteria, think about your own behaviours. Do not try to play political games: colleagues will see through this, and will not appreciate it. Your aims must be to understand and fit in, to be yourself, and to grow yourself.

How will you judge success? University views

- Good feedback from the university supervisor visiting the students.
- Student given appropriate responsibility.
- Good student feedback.
- Recognise and build on the skills that you have, and use them in the future.
- Able to say, 'I got so much out of this'.
- Good feedback from managers.
- Come back to university and be able to promote the organisation with the next set of placement applicants.

How will you judge success? Organisation views

- Know what the key competences required are, and demonstrate them.
- Let your organisation believe 'I am glad that this person is in my team'.
- If you are unhappy, or finding things difficult, speak to your manager or mentor: nip any problems in the bud.
- Be where you need to be on time!
- Keep a note of key projects and situations you have worked on, and examples of the competences which you have demonstrated.
- Participate as widely as you can in the work and social life of your placement organisation.
- Be professional: reflect the culture of the organisation.
- Be willing to take on extra responsibility if required.
- An enquiring student who isn't afraid to ask questions!

6.4 Behaviour and dealing with inappropriate behaviour

Your placement requires very different norms and behaviours from what you may be used to at university. At its simplest, this means looking as though you belong to the organisation in dress and language and always being on time and fully briefed and prepared. But there are wider challenges in your behaviours, and how you can reasonably expect others to behave towards you as well.

Fair performance assessment and workloads

Of course, you should expect fair performance assessment and fair workloads. But there are no objective criteria for these, and they are much more a basis of discussion and, sometimes, negotiation. Line management capability to handle these reviews varies between excellent and unsatisfactory.

Performance assessment is not a one-way process, and you will be expected to have undertaken much of the pre-assessment process beforehand (see also Chapter 8 on reflective learning). Managers will often ask you to undertake a self-assessment as part of the assessment review, as well as giving you their own views. Make sure that you can back up your self-assessment with evidence based on your work objectives, or competences.

Workloads can be very variable, so you will need to take a view over a period of a few weeks about whether you have an abnormally high, or low, workload. A small proportion of placement students describe their workload as high (but nevertheless, enjoyable, fulfilling, and recognised by their managers), but a higher proportion of students report work troughs, when they did not feel there was sufficient to do. Discuss your workload with your manager. If, unusually, workloads are expected to be low for while, it may be a good time to access in-company training in a relevant skill, to start work on your dissertation, or to ask if you can work-shadow another area for a short period. The important thing is to discuss a low workload with your manager, and bring some realistic proposals. Don't sit at your desk feeling and looking bored – your colleagues may not say anything, but will not understand your low activity, and may even resent it if they themselves are busy. Neither does low activity help towards your learning objectives.

What can go wrong on a placement? University experience

Poor evidence of reflective learning, as evidenced in a poor learning journal – the student fails to think through the experience and learning.
Student committing to do something, but then fails to do it.
Placement context changes and student cannot be accommodated.
Student does not attend work consistently.
Mutual purpose of placement never fully understood, even by the end of the placement.

Use of IT and telephones

An organisation's rules and behaviours on the use of IT, the telephone, and (if you are offered one) mobile phones and PDAs do vary. You *must* find out what may be regarded as acceptable behaviour (perhaps a brief phone call to say that you will be late home), and what is not (longer personal phone calls, or any personal phone calls at all; use of emails for personal benefit; social networking sites, etc.).

It may sound obvious – yet doesn't stop people falling into the trap – but filling in time when you are not busy by sending personal emails or making personal phone calls is unacceptable anywhere. Find out what the organisation's rules are and stick to them. Do not base your own conduct on what longer serving colleagues do.

Bullying and harassment

Bullying or harassment towards you or from you towards a colleague will always be treated as unacceptable, and potentially as a serious disciplinary matter. This includes inappropriate behaviours based on gender, sexual orientation, disability, age, ethnicity or religion. You are expected to abide by appropriate standards of behaviours, as well as having the right to be treated appropriately. These behaviours cover physical behaviours (for example, not touching colleagues inappropriately), and verbal conduct (for example, comments or humour). What is regarded as 'inappropriate' is based on how the individual responds to an alleged offensive behaviour, not on any 'objective' criteria. So these must set the standard for your own behaviour and what you can expect from your colleagues. Most organisations have anti-bullying/harassment polices, and these will cover conduct and remarks, especially when based on gender, sexual orientation, ethnicity, age, disability, or religious belief. If you feel that you have been subjected to bullying or harassment, you should speak first to your manager.

Your conduct and integrity

High standards of conduct and integrity during your internship will be taken for granted by your host organisation. Getting this right may not gain you any additional points, but getting it wrong will seriously derail, and possibly ruin, your placement.

Make sure you understand your organisation's most important rules: these are usually included in the disciplinary procedure, and will make clear the formal rules that will apply in the workplace.

Remember, too, your conduct outside the workplace. If you have enjoyed a night out, that's fine. But you will be expected to arrive at work the next day fresh and alert. If you think that your colleagues are interested in your exploits of the night before, distinguish whether it is the exploits themselves which are the centre of their attention ... or their bemusement about what you are saying about yourself as an individual. Behaviours within an organisation will be very different from university norms.

In the very rare circumstances when placement students actually break an organisation's rules, they will usually be managed under a Disciplinary Procedure. If this happens to you, find a colleague or union representative who can assist you with this process.

Where to go for help

Workloads

Many problems at work will come from a breakdown in communication or expectations, and can be straightforwardly resolved by speaking to the relevant person. If you are having any problems at work with your assessments or your workload, you should first speak to your line manager. Before you do so, make sure that you have the facts ready, and have taken the time to consider 'the other side of the story' – for example, have you understood the position clearly in the first place?

If you are concerned about how your manager will respond, speak to your mentor first.

Inappropriate behaviour

If you believe that you have been subjected to inappropriate behaviour, you should speak to your manager, who will explain how you may take your complaint forward within the organisation's formal policies.

Domestic

It is unlikely that your host workplace will have facilities in place to resolve domestic issues such as finding accommodation, etc. However, employees in larger organisations often have informal networks or information sources for temporary accommodation, car share schemes, etc., so it is worthwhile to enquire about these.

Larger organisations will sometimes have confidential help schemes for staff. These are usually based on telephone advice support from professional staff. If you have a personal problem, it is well worth considering using these helplines for professional and confidential support.

University

Of course, your university should also be advised if you are having problems at work. However, whilst your university will have seen most problems, and be able to advise you who to talk to, it is usually quicker and easier if you can sort these out with your host organisation directly.

6.5 Summary

Even if you have had student work experience before, your placement is likely to be a very different experience. You will be treated more seriously by your organisation, who, in turn, will expect you to behave more professionally too.

Make a point of understanding the required standards, and keep a note of them in your learning journal (Chapter 8) for ease of reference.

Settling in quickly and smoothly will enable you to make a good start on the work and learning experience from your placement – and we start to look at those in more detail in Chapter 7.

Checklist

1 Make sure that you have your P45 ready on your first day of service. You may also need to show proof of eligibility to work so bring your passport to work too on the first day.
2 Understand *how* your organisational performance will be judged and assessed – both work objectives and competence development.
3 Understand *when* your organisational performance will be assessed – put the date in your diary, and, about 10 days beforehand, put a time in your diary to prepare for the assessments.
4 Check the training and development planned by the host organisation.
5 Understand the key formal requirements of the organisation (time keeping; who to call if you cannot attend work; etc.).

6.6 Further information

Futher reading

Cameron, S. (2005) *The MBA Handbook*. Harlow: FT/Prentice-Hall.

Not ready for an MBA yet? Don't be put off by title, an excellent book on study and working at the same time, with lots of practical guidance.

Useful contacts

HM Revenue and Customs, for details about tax, and how to get your tax code:
www.hmrc.gov.uk

Directgov, for a wide range of information including tax and social security benefits:
www.direct.gov.uk./en/index.htm

Financial Service Authority *Money Made Clear*:
www.fsa.gov.uk/guides

Chapter 7

Key Practical Skills

Chapter contents

A key skill you developed as a student, and will certainly need to enhance in your career, is how to make the most of your time, and balance conflicting priorities. You will also need some key skills in the workplace which you may not have used to any great extent in your studies.

As students move from university to organisational life, both they and the organisations they work for will report on the culture shock evident in moving from lecture/seminar environments to a full working day, five days a week. At its simplest, it is important that you get to work in time, and attend meetings and so on on time. These are basic to workplace discipline. But your work placement should teach you other critically important management skills as well, such as writing reports, arranging meetings, managing your time, IT and project management.

7.1 Writing reports

Whilst on your placement, you are likely to be asked to prepare short reports and to contribute to longer reports, so it is important to be able to approach this with confidence about their structure and content.

Check the style preferred for reports in your organisation, and follow that. If there is no expected style, your report could cover the following general conventions on style and content.

> ### Report style
>
> 1 Introduction
> 2 Background
> 3 Options for the future: with arguments for and arguments against
> 4 Proposed way forward and supporting rational
> 5 Cost/income impacts
> 6 Timescales
> 7 What next
> 8 Conclusion
> 9 Appendices for additional information

Before you write, check when the report is due for submission, and try to beat that deadline – not only will this show that you are motivated, but at a very practical level it will also reduce the time pressures on you when the inevitable amendments are suggested.

Check the length of the required report – if no length is suggested, try to ensure that routine reports or briefs are contained within two sides of an A4 sheet.

Be prepared for your report to be written and re-written, especially if it is going to senior management. Learn from the style/content changes which may be made to your original draft, and don't take any changes personally! It is much easier to comment on/redraft a report once it has been started than to originate one yourself. So, even if your report is very different from your first draft, be assured that you made the big contribution in getting the process started.

7.2 Arranging meetings

Fixing meetings

You may be asked to organise meetings ... you may also wonder why you are doing a degree to organise a meeting, and even why it is mentioned in this book! Nevertheless, it is an important basic skill for any employee. Classic mistakes in arranging meetings may be too embarrassing for many of your colleagues to discuss, but the authors are certainly aware of some howlers here – such as sending delegates to the 'right' room in the wrong building, or arranging complex interview days, with highly paid assessors, but failing to invite the candidates who were to be assessed. So if you are asked to fix a meeting, good attention to detail and using some of the following tips should help you.

- Rooms – may get busy early, so book early, and book a series of these if several meeting dates are planned.

- Agenda – should be circulated a week in advance to attendees, together with any pre-circulated papers which need to be read beforehand.

- Equipment – may need to be ordered, so do check. If data projectors are to be used for presentations, make sure you know how laptops or PCs are connected and who to contact on the day in case of failure.

- Catering – get this wrong at your peril! But make sure, too, that you check that your manager's cost centre can take any internal charging.

- Attendees – it sounds obvious, but do ensure that ALL attendees, including any visiting presenters, have a copy of the agenda.

- Notes – If you are asked to take notes don't try to take down everything that is said, unless you are taking down notes for a specialised reason (for example, witness reports, or at a disciplinary or grievance hearing). Capture the essence of what is being said. Most importantly, ensure that you have recorded the action points accurately for the meeting: who is responsible for delivering an agreed action, and by what date. The longer after a meeting that you try to write the notes into an official format, the worse it can be. So, when you know you are at a meeting, add another hour into your calendar immediately after the meeting, so as to keep free the time required to do this. If you cannot do this, ensure that you have these written up within 24 hours – even if it means doing them at home. Check the notes with the manager leading the meeting before you release them. Learn from any changes to what you have written and don't take changes personally – instead, consider how and why the meeting chair may have preferred to use a different emphasis or tone.

7.3 Managing your time

Managing your own time is a key skill to develop. Many professionals and managers with long experience may say that they still haven't got it right, but your placement will be more effective if you can start it with good time management practices in place.

It is probably inevitable during your placement that you will have times when you have too much work, about the right amount of work, and sometimes too little. Having a clear idea of your work objectives will help you smooth out any peaks and troughs. If you find that you have too little to do during some periods, speak to your manager first, then check if your colleagues need any help. If you still feel under-employed, see whether you can undertake any online training available in the organisation.

Heavy workloads should not be a consistent part of your placement experience, but may occur during phases of work.

If your workload is greater or less than expected, you may experience stress. If so, try to step back and think about this as part of your placement learning experience too.

Overall, good personal management of your time, constructively smoothing out periods of higher and lower work activity, and being a good team member supporting (or accept support from) others are important parts of your placement experience, and good material for reflection in your learning journal.

7.4 IT

There are three key areas which you need to be aware of in your placement organisation:

- *Using networked systems effectively.* In many organisations, networked systems are the primary ways in which teams work together, so it is important that you quickly become efficient in their use. Understand how networked systems are used as early on as possible, including shared drives for file handling and networked diary systems. If these systems are not intuitive in their own right, or you are not familiar with them, ask a colleague for help.

- *Working with software packages specific to your role.* It may seem tempting to try to pick up learning software as you go along, but if you do so, you will often miss major areas of functionality and are likely to work inefficiently with a package. So once you have settled into your role, be proactive and ask for early training on any software which may be specialised for your role.

- *Organisational IT security and use regulations.* You *must* find out about your organisation's IT security and use regulations and follow them precisely. Media reports remind us how critically important it should be to avoid laptops being stolen, data storage systems being lost or stolen with confidential information available, sensitive information not being encrypted, and individual cases of disciplinary action taking place for using work-based IT systems to access private or inappropriate use during working hours such as social networking sites.

Make sure that you follow the IT rules, and not what you may see other colleagues doing on the system. Mis-use of IT is treated seriously by organisations, but often there is no obvious monitoring or action until individual cases are followed up, often through the Disciplinary Procedure.

You will be held responsible for any activity undertaken on your log-in code. If you have been fairly relaxed as a student in sharing log-in passwords, do not let this happen in your placement organisation, even if you see other colleagues doing this on an informal basis. When you walk away from your computer screen, ensure that you have logged off. At all times, ensure that your use of the IT system is appropriate and in line with the organisation's IT policy.

7.5 Project management

Many placement students will find themselves asked to run, or participate in, a project during their placement, so an understanding of project terminologies and approaches will help you through this. Ideally, see if you can do a short project management course at university, or in your placement organisation, since effective project management skills are an essential part of modern business life.

In the meantime, this overview of projects will help you to understand.

When is work 'a project'?

The work you have been asked to do could be described as a 'project' (rather than 'business as usual') if it:

- Involves a one-off assignment (for example, organising an event, producing a training package, a marketing campaign, the implementation of new IT, etc.).

- Has a clear start time and a clear completion time.

- Involves a wide range of co-ordination and control activities.

What are the key stages in managing a project?

There are various techniques for identifying the key stages of a project, but they may be summarised as follows:

- *Define the project*

    1 Define the business need for the project.

        a) What is needed?

        b) Why is it needed?

    2 Prepare a business case, explaining why the project should go ahead.

        a) How will the project be delivered?

        b) Who needs to be involved at each stage?

        c) When will it start and finish?

        d) How much will it cost?

        e) What are the business/income/other benefits?

- *Design the project process*

    3   Decide how the project will be supported and supplied ('Procurement Strategy')*.

    4   Invite tenders to perform the project*.

    5   Decide and award the contract for the project*.

- *Deliver the project*

    6   Manage the implementation of the project.

        a)   Who will manage the project?

        b)   How will quality, cost, and time be managed?

        c)   How will stakeholders be managed?

        d)   How will on-going risks be identified and managed?

    7   Close the project.

        a)   When and how will you know that the project has been completed, and successfully handed over to 'business as usual'?

- *Develop the process*

    8   Undertake a Post Implementation Review (PIR).

        a)   Review all aspects of how the project went in time, quality, cost, and for stakeholders.

        b)   What went well, and how/why did this happen? How can it be repeated another time?

        c)   What did not go so well, and why? How might this be avoided/mitigated next time?

        d)   What has been your individual role in this project? What have you done well/not so well, and learned for next time?

(* shown for completeness, but for smaller scale projects, this is likely to be managed and supported in-house.)

How will the project be judged?

It is very important that you know how the project will be judged, and the success criteria will need to be agreed with the person who originally commissioned the work (the 'project sponsor'). In agreeing success criteria, you should take into account:

- *How will the success be judged?* See sections below on time/cost/quality and stakeholders.

- *Should a project specification be written?* For larger projects, it is worthwhile to set out all the factors which will impact on the project and develop a project specification. Smaller projects may not need this, but it would be good experience to develop a project specification if you have time.

- *Is there any doubt or ambiguity about what has to be achieved?* ... and are all sides aware of the risks and obstacles which may occur?

- *Are the targets clear?* ... and are they written in SMART terms, with objectives which are Specific, Measurable, Agreed, Realistic, and Timed?

The quality/time/cost triangle

It is important to remember the quality/time/cost triangle in project management: each of these needs to be in balance, and if one is out of balance, then the other two are likely to suffer. For example if timescales are shortened for a project, and quality must remain the same, then costs are likely to increase. Similarly, if costs and timescales to deliver are shortened, then quality is likely to suffer.

Being clear about stakeholders

Stakeholders can be defined as anyone concerned with how an organisation operates, and who is going to be affected by an organisational change or programme of changes (Huczynski and Buchanan, 2007: 599). Who are the key stakeholders in your project (for example, other departments, colleagues, third party suppliers, customers, trades unions)? What power/influence do they have, and how will you manage this? Who are the end users of the project? How will these end users be represented in your work as it is being designed?

Alert to change management skills

If your project will require a change of work behaviours or routines, bear in mind the change management requirements. Research (for example, Kotter, 1995) has demonstrated that projects fail less often because they were poorly designed technically, but more often that the change management implications – and critically how people will adjust and readjust to required changes – have not been sufficiently taken into consideration. So ensure that your project gives attention to any required communication, training, and support as it is implemented.

Managing the risks

Think through the risks in delivering your project successfully to the quality, time and cost standards required – what can get in the way, such as stakeholders changing their minds, budgets being cut halfway through the project, etc. Prepare a project risk assessment, and consider:

- The nature of the risk (for example legal, cost, stakeholder, etc.).
- The possible consequences of the risk were it to happen.
- How the risk can be mitigated.
- What action has been/will be taken to manage the risk.

Learning from project completion

At the end of the project, it is good practice to do a post implementation review (PIR) to understand what went well, what might have been done differently, and what has been learned for future projects. This usually involves bringing together the key stakeholders, and reviewing the project's outcomes against what was actually planned.

It is not unusual for organisations to skip the PIR, especially in the case of smaller projects which have been judged to have been successful, and, ironically, not worthwhile to review *because* they have been successful! However, even if you cannot undertake a formal PIR on completion of a project, do undertake your own reflection of good and development lessons learned, as these will certainly be important for your personal development and may also be valuable in the reflective learning which your university or professional body may require.

Watch the project time and costs!

Once you are involved with a project, be aware that the time you spend on it, and the costs to the organisation, increase very rapidly once the project has been commissioned; so if you are responsible for cost tracking, make sure that you have good systems in place. If you are part of the project team, be prepared to make time in your diary for the workload which most projects entail.

Top tips from students: what I'd have done differently

- Set myself objectives beforehand, then strive to achieve them.
- Prepared myself for drastic changes in my lifestyle compared with university.
- Thought more about the type of organisation where I wanted to have my placement, and where it might lead to.
- Would have sent off more speculative applications.
- Prepared better: taken some time to understand the business first.

(Cont'd)

- Discussed with my company what I wanted to get out of the placement.
- Gotten more sleep!
- Been more forward with some of my ideas; been more vocal on dull days.
- If something does start to go wrong, I would speak to my manager; not ignore it, or be underhand.

7.6 Your learning journal

Remember that all the activities in this section – how you tackled them, the outcomes, what you might have done differently, and why – are excellent material for your Learning Journal.

7.7 Further information

On management generally

Kennedy, C. (2002) *Guide to the Management Gurus*. London: Random House Books.

Don't tell your tutor that you have found this book! Easily digestible chapters on 40+ key management thinkers, across a wide range of business disciplines. Most chapters only five to ten pages long. Great way to extend your management knowledge across a range of disciplines, whilst you see them in action in the workplace. But do find original sources for your written work.

On projects

Maylor, H. (2003) *Project Management*. Harlow: Pearson Education.

If you are involved in a larger scale project, a good overall guide to project management; similar other introductory books are also available.

Professional bodies / associations
Association of Project Management (APM) www.apm.org.uk
Project Management Institute (PMI) www.pmi.org
Projects in Controlled Environments (PRINCE2) www.prince2.co.uk

Project planning software
Various kinds of project planning software support are available, for example, Microsoft Office Project. This helps detailed planning and

gives very professional project charts – but make sure you understand the principles first, and don't become blinded by the software.

On time management

A diary

Sounds obvious, but if you haven't got one already, get one now. As well as day-to-day work, remember to include key deliverable dates, such as reports for your placement organisation, reports for university, and key stages in researching and writing your dissertation.

Shared diaries (e.g. Microsoft Outlook)

Many organisations use computer-based diary systems, with shared access; other people can book into your diary, and you may be able to book into theirs too. Find out quickly what system is being used, and become proficient in its use. If you find it difficult to keep track of times and dates of appointments without hard copy, print a copy of the day, or, more economically and environmentally friendly, week ahead view.

Notepad and pen

Always have a notepad and pen with you – if you have an idea, make a note of it straight away; if you agree to do something, make a note of it – then transfer this to your diary back at your desk.

Checklist

1 Understand how to use your organisation's online diary (for example, Outlook).
2 Think about getting a paper-based diary, and use it daily.
3 Ensure that you understand your organisation's IT policy and rules.
4 Become proficient as early as possible in using IT packages – avoid guessing your way through, and ask for appropriate training.
5 Look for opportunities to volunteer for assignments and work, but make sure that your other work and university commitments will not be damaged.
6 Don't forget to keep your Learning Journal up to date and to use reflective learning (Chapter 8).

Chapter 8

Learning from Your Placement

Chapter contents

8.1 Introduction to learning on your placement

opening sentence

Continuous learning is important throughout your career. There will be few times in your career where learning will be the most important part of your daily working life, but your placement is one such time. You will be required to deliver work goals, but your placement is very much about learning too. So in this chapter we will consider how to make the most of any learning opportunities.

First, it is important to focus on the kinds of things which you will be learning, and the ways in which you will learn them, which will often be different from university learning. In Chapter 1, we saw that employers often bemoan the fact that graduates do not have the right skills and competences to be of value in the workplace. And yet, with a degree, they clearly have levels of knowledge which at least form a platform for their working lives, and in some cases may exceed what they need in the workplace. So what is happening here?

Your ability to work at university or in the workplace depends on an appropriate balance of your knowledge, skills, and competences, but a different level of emphasis is required in the workplace, as shown in Table 8.1.

Table 8.1   Knowledge, competence, skill balance and university workplace emphasis

Area of learning	Definition	Examples	University emphasis	Workplace emphasis
Knowledge/ theory		Knowledge of technical processes, such as law, accounting standards and processes, project management techniques, and so on	High, and critical to overall assessment	Important, especially where knowledge is central to a professional role Emphasis on knowledge/theory alone less critical than at university Degree class requirements more often a surrogate for assessing competences, determination, and ability to deliver results, rather than showing the theory/knowledge gained
Competence	The ability to apply knowledge and skills to a required level of performance		Assumed levels of competence. Knowledge and skills to write and present effectively more important	High importance
Skill		Writing Numeracy IT skills Presentation ability	Important	Important

8.2 Seeing the linkages in learning

An important area to focus on in your placement is seeing and understanding the linkages in learning. Some students fail to do this, and therefore see separate learning events as not joined up any way – for example, viewing learning SAP accounting methods for work, finance theory for university, and competence development, such as managing the customer relationship, as of little practical relevance, other than for the next job interview.

Of course, the reality is that all this learning is linked, and needs to be seen as a whole: learning SAP is important for day-to-day process work, understanding the theory of finance is important for a deeper understanding of financial management and future career development, but none of this is of value unless you can operate effectively with internal and external customers. There is a difference in emphasis between what a university regards as successful and what is required to be successful in the workplace. These differences may account for why employers talk publicly about the shortage of graduates with 'the competences and skills needed for the workplace' as we saw in Chapter 1. The value in your placement is that you will have the chance to develop competences and skills, as well as extend your knowledge. However, this does require a fresh look at what we learn, as well as how we learn it. Therefore, this chapter will discuss techniques to help you make the most of all your learning opportunities whilst on your placement.

At university, your competences – the range of behaviours required to get the job done, and your skills, your ability to use IT, make presentations – are important, but less important than your theoretical knowledge. In an organisational setting, your competences and skills to get the job done will often be considered to be more important than your theoretical knowledge.

It is important that you see the whole of your workplace learning as integrated: you are developing further theoretical knowledge, your workplace competences, and your workplace skills. The techniques for doing this may be different, but the outcomes in developing you as a 'whole person' are the same.

This difference in how you learn is one of the key reasons why you are doing a placement. The emphasis shifts from learning by reading and listening, to learning by doing. But 'doing' is not sufficient to learn effectively: for this to happen, we need to reflect on what we have done, and adjust our future behaviours. If this action, reflection, and adjustment do not happen, or if we skip stages in the cycle, then we are not learning, but are instead carrying on doing things the wrong way. Kolb and colleagues (1984) refer to this process of learning style as a cycle.

8.3 Learning journal

Whether or nor your university requires it, and irrespective of the length of your placement, you are strongly advised to keep a Learning Journal. This is the right place to keep notes on all aspects of your placement. It can be kept in any format which you will feel most comfortable with paper based, or electronically.

Reflective learners (see Learning Styles, pp. 105–6) are more likely be comfortable keeping a journal, but experience shows that all students need to be encouraged to get into the habit of writing down brief summaries of what they are learning on their placements. You should set aside time in your diary to update your journal at least once a week.

Student tips on learning journals

- I keep a journal. I write up brief notes of what happens in the day or the week – what I've learned, how I feel, what I still need to do. It's surprising how you develop over time, and what you can even forget.
- I meant to keep a journal, but didn't get round to it – I regret that now.

Your journal is there for you to keep notes on anything that is relevant to your placement – from basic facts to recording your observations, and feelings, about your placement. If you were managing the organisation, what would you do differently and why? What do you particularly like about the way the organisation works, and why? What working and management style would you personally wish to adopt? What are the advantages and disadvantages of your preferred approach and what alternatives should you consider?

Your Learning Journal will also help you to improve your understanding of how different aspects of your learning link together.

8.4 Emotional intelligence

The dynamics of the workplace, where individuals and teams strive to meet performance and stakeholder requirements, can become a cauldron of personality stressors. Towards the end of the twentieth century, research was undertaken into why US business school graduates, often with similar levels of intelligence (as measured by IQ), had very different levels of personal and business success later in life. One set of theories developed in this area suggested that intellect alone was not enough to explain these different levels of attainment. Instead, it was also necessary to consider emotional intelligence (EQ).

EQ was originally defined as:

the ability to monitor one's own and others' feelings and emotions, to discriminate among them, and to use this information to guide one's thinking and actions. (Salovey and Mayer, 1989)

Whilst the evidence for the importance of EQ may not yet be clear cut, the claims for its importance are less restrained. Indeed, by 1998, Daniel Goleman, who is perhaps the most eminent proponent of the value of EQ, referred to it as being even more important than IQ (1988: 5).

Goleman's work looked at EQ from two perspectives – social competence and personal competence. These may be further sub-divided as follows:

Social competence

- Empathy

- Organisational awareness

- Service orientation

- Social skills

- Developing others

- Leadership

- Communication

- Building bonds

- Teamwork collaboration.

Personal competence

- Self-aware

- Emotionally self-aware: know effects of emotions

- Accurate self-assessment

- Self-confidence

- Self-management

- Self-control

- Trustworthy

- Conscientious

- Adaptable

- Achievement orientation

- Initiative.

As you navigate your progress through your placement organisation, it is worthwhile to have these perspectives in mind as you observe the behaviours of other colleagues, especially managers, and seek to understand how positive and negative examples relate to organisation and/or work success. Try to distinguish between short-term 'wins', and longer term, sustainable, success. Keep examples of each in your learning log.

It is also worthwhile to develop a realistic view of your own social and personal competence – where you show strengths, and where you may need to develop further. Keep a note of these in your learning log as well.

8.5 Learning styles

It is helpful to have a clear view of your own learning styles. Understanding your learning styles will help you to understand how and when you are most likely to learn … and, just as importantly, recognise other ways in which you could learn, but may be less receptive to doing so, and therefore losing a useful opportunity to extend your understanding and knowledge.

Honey and Mumford (1986, 2006) identified four main typologies of learning style: Theorist, Activist, Pragmatist and Reflector. These learning style types are summarised in Table 8.2 over the page. During your placement, it is a good idea to try out other ways of learning – perhaps experiment with learning styles and ways of doing things where you may feel less comfortable. As you do so, you will widen your learning base and may find different approaches which are equally effective as your preferred styles, as well as develop your managing styles.

8.6 Working in teams

Most organisational activity is undertaken within and between teams, so a good understanding of team working is essential when developing your personal effectiveness. In this section, we will look at:

- Your personality – how you are likely to interact with team members.

- The roles people have within teams.

- How teams interact with each other.

Your personality – how you are likely to interact with team members

What type of personality you have, and how you prefer to work, will clearly impact on how you get on with people with a similar outlook, a complementary outlook, or with whom you simply clash.

The roles people have within teams

Team roles does not just refer to the formal function you have within a team (for example, marketing assistant, HR assistant, etc.), but also to

Table 8.2 **Learning styles**

Style	People with this style tend to ...	Alternative learning approaches to consider
Theorist	Be organised, and to like clarity and structure. Analytical, methodical and uses critical thinking. Also logical problem solving.	Try to be more innovative or creative at times. Try working in situations which you may not have previously encountered or read about. Involve others in your thinking – what perspectives do they bring? Speak up more at meetings.
Activist	Prefer to learn by doing things, and settle down to work quickly and happily. Appear enthusiastic in group situations.	Likely to find it particularly hard to keep that all-important learning journal and to keep up with reading! Think and plan before you do something. What theory, process or policy should apply here? Have you thought through carefully the impact of what you are doing? (reflection) Ensure that you sustain your interest through to a successful completion.
Pragmatist	Be practical. Enjoy the real life environment. See the connections between theory and practice. Be realistic and good problem solvers.	Could develop more reflective thinking styles. May find it difficult at times to be really creative. Don't forget to maintain some reading during your placement! Another style which is likely to find keeping the learning journal a challenge!
Reflector	Think deeply about things, listen carefully to others, strong in reflection and learning. Not be comfortable starting something without having thought about it carefully first.	Actively involve others by discussing your thoughts with them. Don't always aim for perfection. Speak up more at meetings – try to make at least three significant contributions in that next meeting.

Table 8.3 **Team role descriptions**

Team Role	Contribution	Allowable weaknesses
Plant	Creative, imaginative, unorthodox. Solves difficult problems.	Ignores incidentals. Too pre-occupied to communicate effectively.
Resource Investigator	Extrovert, enthusiastic, communicative. Explores opportunities. Develops contacts.	Over-optimistic. Loses interest once an initial enthusiasm has passed.
Co-ordinator	Mature, confident, a good chairperson. Clarifies goals, promotes decision making, delegates well.	Can be seen as manipulative. Offloads personal work.
Shaper	Challenging, dynamic, thrives on pressure. The drive and courage to overcome obstacles.	Prone to provocation. Offends people's feelings.
Monitor Evaluator	Sober, strategic and discerning. Sees all opinions. Judges accurately.	Lacks drive and the ability to inspire others.
Teamworker	Co-operative, mild, perceptive and diplomatic Listens, builds, avoids friction.	Indecisive in crunch situations.
Implementer	Disciplined, reliable, conservative and efficient. Turns ideas into practical actions.	Somewhat inflexible. Slow to respond to new possibilities.
Completer Finisher	Painstaking, conscientious, anxious. Searches out errors and omissions. Polishes and perfects.	Inclined to worry unduly. Reluctant to delegate.
Specialist	Single-minded, self-starting, dedicated. Provides knowledge and skills in rare supply.	Contributes on only a narrow front. Dwells on technicalities.

how you are likely to perform in a team role, irrespective of your formal organisational job title.

Belbin (1981) identified the following nine types of roles which individuals may adopt within teams.

For teams to work effectively each of these team types must be present – for example, there is little point having highly creative people, great leadership skills, etc., and then finding that work is not done at all, or not done on time. Equally, individuals will tend to have a mix of individually dominant team styles, and less dominant styles.

As you observe team meetings, consider the respective roles of team members, and how results are being achieved. As you do so, also think about your own style within a team – in which roles are you most or least comfortable, and why? To develop your effectiveness within the team, which other roles should you seek to develop? These are important areas for your Personal Development Plan, and also for reflective learning in your learning journal.

How teams interact with each other

Healthy competition between teams can be productive, and can also be fun. But too often, it can break down into inter-team competition and rivalry within the organisation, rather than team work to beat the competition. A lot of the time this can apply particularly between teams who rely on each other's interdependence to get the job done. Here are some illustrations of what previous placement students experienced.

> I worked in the HR shared services area. Line and even HR managers never seemed to understand the time it took to ensure that references and background security checks were completed before someone could start work.

> In change projects, we had some really good people, but our work was hampered because the people in procurement were so slow in supporting us. So we never really talked to them.

> The trouble is, the people in planet x [head office] just don't seem to understand what it's like here in the branch, working with customers.

There may well be issues and problems which need to be addressed in each of these illustrations, but it is highly unlikely that the full blame rests in each case with 'the other department'. So it is worth understanding how this can happen, and what organisations may be able to do to manage it.

However, each of these quotes above are examples of 'group think' – this concept has been widely researched in organisations and has been defined as:

> The term given to the pressure that highly cohesive groups exert on their members for uniform and acceptable decisions that actually reduces their capacity to make effective decisions. (Janis, 1972)

We can see examples of group think in our everyday lives. Sports teams, ever optimistic about their capability over rivals, and yet they still lose; excessive commitment to the strength of 'my organisation or brand', without seeing the value in competitors or niche players; my university is better than your's, because …

Working well and effectively within a cohesive and high performing team is important to individual, team, and organisational success. But the big risks of over-reliance on group think include a failure:

- To think through and analyse problems sufficiently clearly.

- To check all information sources objectively – for example, with an external benchmark or the use of external advisers; even a failure to trust internal advisers who are not part of the group.

- To have a second look at options which may have been rejected previously, but now, for different reasons, may be viable.

- To consider facts objectively, rejecting external information as flawed or invalid when it conflicts with the group think.

- To assess risk sufficiently.

So strong team cohesion is important, but also has its downsides. Team leaders can redress some of the negative effects of group think by using various techniques, such as:

- Asking some team members to adopt a 'devil's advocate' stance when discussing plans.

- Encouraging each person in the group to think 'outside the box' and to not just accept ideas without thinking about them critically.

- Using 360 degree feedback and customer survey techniques to see how others see us, and the service we provide.

- Including 'mystery shop' competitors and feedback to the team as to what others may do better than us.

On your placement, remember that it is not your role to change the world where this is not asked of you. Your role is to fit in within the team and be a valued team player. However, do observe and understand what may be happening with group think and behaviours within and between departments and with competitor organisations. And if this was your own business, what would you do to resolve it?? You can record some of this material in your learning journal, and within your personal development plan.

Getting the most from your placement: university views

Take reflective self-improvement seriously.

Use a learning journal to record your learning as your placement progresses.

Make sure you are properly organised: know when and where you need to be (diary); know what you need to do (clear work objectives).

8.7 Personal development planning

Why it is important

Good personal development planning is essential to make the most of your placement. But there are many reasons why you may give it second place, against more immediate pressures such as learning your day-to-day role, not knowing what to include with your personal development plan, being too busy, being too tired, or simply finding it an irksome chore. However, the breadth of experience and opportunity you have in your placement will only be maximised if you approach this methodically.

You may be given a format for your personal development plan by your host organisation, or your university. If this is not possible, a wide range of professional bodies has formats for their members, so go to the Continuing Professional Development site of the professional body you hope to join on graduation, and use a plan format from that organisation.

And if all this fails, then put together your own plan format! The key steps are to plan your development, to undertake your development, and then review what you have done and re-plan for the future. SMART objectives are required in your planning – not vague and unrealistic promises to yourself, which will disappear as quickly as last year's New Year resolutions.

Tips for managing your personal development

It is easy to overlook the active management of your personal development – some people expect learning to 'come naturally'. For others it may be a chore, or can appear to be irrelevant. This is more likely to be because of your personal learning style, rather than the discipline you are studying at university, or the environment in which you are working. Tips for how to manage your personal development more effectively are:

- Regularly review what you are doing, the things you have encountered, and the things which you recognise you still need to learn. Spend half an hour a week on this activity, and diarise when and where you will do it.

- Write down what you have learned and still need to learn – facts, views, when you have succeeded, and how that was achieved.

- Do an honest self-reflection when an assignment has been difficult – how and why did this happen? How could you have handled stakeholders differently? Were you adequately prepared yourself? Did you have the necessary skills, and resources to do the work? Were the requirements sufficiently clear?

What to include in your personal development plan

Remember that you are developing three types of learning in your placement:

- Your theoretical, professional and academic knowledge – the things which will be of greatest value to you for university and professional development reasons.
- Your competences – the behaviours which an organisation looks at to assess your capability to achieve the required results in the organisation.
- Your skills – such as IT, project management techniques, presentation to large groups, etc.

It is important that you see these as part of an overall learning plan. They are not individual elements for different audiences. They are an integrated part of you developing your CV, employability, and potential – your personal employment brand. Remember also that your personal development plan needs to achieve two key aims: to ensure your effectiveness in your current role; and to provide a springboard for your future career. The box format of Personal Development Formats may not be the best place to start here, so we suggest an alternative approach, the Holistic Personal Development Plan to consider where you are in your role now, and what your key strengths are, your development areas in technical/professional/academic knowledge; what you would really like to do in three to five years' time, and what your personal/family and friends' priorities are. These can be mapped together as shown in Figure 8.2 over the page.

Your university or organisation may be able to give you guidance or instructions about what it requires you to have in your personal development plan. Obviously, you need to follow this, but also think about the wider issues in your personal development which we discussed in Chapters 6–8. Organisations may also focus more on the learning they think you need to achieve during the next 12 months, or for the period of your placement. But you need a wider horizon too – what kind of things do you want to be doing in the next three to five years? What do you need to do now in order to prepare for them?

Think also about *how* your placement organisation works. Read the sections in this book about leadership and management: how do you see these standards being applied? Read up about group working: again, how is this applied in practical situations, what are the consequences, and how might things be done differently? And think about yourself as an individual as well: not simply about your evolving academic and professional knowledge, but also about how your style interacts with other colleagues: what works well, what not so well, and what you can do personally to build on your strengths and address some of your development areas.

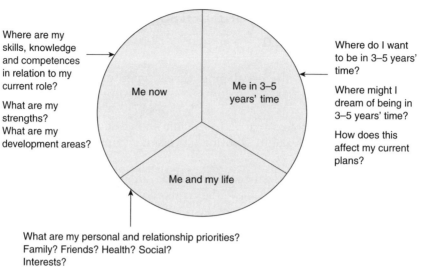

Where are my skills, knowledge and competences in relation to my current role?

What are my strengths?
What are my development areas?

Me now

Me in 3–5 years' time

Me and my life

Where do I want to be in 3–5 years' time?

Where might I dream of being in 3–5 years' time?

How does this affect my current plans?

What are my personal and relationship priorities? Family? Friends? Health? Social? Interests?

Figure 8.2   **Personal development learning format (Holistic Personal Development Plans © 2008 Peoplevalued Partnership Ltd)**

Personal development plan formats

Check first whether your university, professional body, or organisation has a personal development format which you are required to use. If they do not, a simple format to use is illustrated in Table 8.4. But what is more important than the format which you use, is to make sure that your personal development gets a regular and systematic review. On your placement, you should update this at least every four weeks.

8.8 Using in-house learning resources

On the job training

Your placement will almost certainly be packed with learning opportunities – both from your placement organisation, as well as from requirements from your university. But much of the training will also be undertaken at your place of work, and as part of your day-to-day activity. Research (CIPD, 2008) has shown that this 'on the job training' is both the most popular training, and the most useful. You will make greatest use of this training if you also combine it with the reflective learning approach discussed in this chapter, and keep track of what you are learning, and your response to it, within your learning journal.

In-house courses

Once you are in your placement organisation, you will have a great chance to use in-house learning facilities to develop your usefulness to

Table 8.3 Sample personal development format

Name			Plan for period	
			October–January	
What do I want to learn?	How could I do this?	What will I do?	What did I learn?	How can I apply this?
(Don't forget, this needs to cover academic/ professional skills; your competence development; and your skills development)	(What learning options do you have? Reading? Coaching? e-learning? Course? Job shadow? On the job training? Face to face training?)	(Ensure that you write this in SMART terms – Specific action; Measurable, Agreed (does your manager need to sign off?); Realistic; and Timed)	(Review the learning after you have completed it)	
Review my learning styles	Complete learning styles questionnaire; discuss with mentor	Research learning styles in October	Strong on theory and activist; weak reflection score	Consider ways to increase reflection; make sure 30 minutes a week set aside to update learning journal
Be more confident in group presentations	Ask for feedback from manager	Do e-learning presentation skills course on 15 November Offer to present customer review figures to next meeting in December		Find other ways to get more learning
Prepare for placement tutor meetings	Diarise meetings now (or e-mail tutor to see when dates planned)	Arrange sessions for November and February; Diarise two weeks beforehand to prepare reports, etc., for meeting		Time management and readiness for tutor

(Cont'd)

Table 8.3

Name	October–January	Plan for period
Progress dissertation meetings	Estimate timetable and write to tutor to suggest meeting times	Request meetings for November, February, and April
		Expect to do most in-company research in Feb and March, so speak to manager to arrange	Make sure my dissertation is written and submitted on time
			Improve overall academic performance and chance of success
Find two mentors in the organisation to help me	Not sure; speak to manager at next 1:1 at end of October	Make sure I have mentorship arranged by mid November, and have met them by end of November	Meet about every five weeks, or as required, to understand progress and put learning into context
Learn Dreamweaver software	Spend time with designer to watch and do some tasks	Try to complete before year end	For future use; offer to cover during holidays or staff absences
	Request to attend in-company training		

your placement organisation, and in doing so, you can enhance your CV and future employability.

Good examples of the types of learning you might expect are:

- Accounting systems.

- Practical customer/client services skills.

- Project management skills.

- HR software packages.

- Selling skills.

- Career development skills.

- Software training, to enhance skills which you may already have, or may develop further, such as project management, Dreamweaver, database management, etc.

Many organisations, especially the larger ones, are increasingly using e-learning (computer or web-based learning), or blended solutions, with a combination of e-learning and more conventional learning, such as face to face training. Once you have settled into the workplace, become familiar with the learning facilities available and spot courses which you might like to access later, and discuss with your manager when/how it may be appropriate to access this training.

Professional and business journals

Many organisations take out regular subscriptions to professional and business journals. It is a good idea to see what is available, and to get yourself on the circulation if possible. If you do not already do so, get a quality newspaper once or twice a week, and take some time to read the business sections.

Get a feel for what is happening in the wider business world in your area. What impact does it have ... or not have ... on your organisation? why? How is your organisation responding?

Planning your training

Good training experiences should be planned, and should fit in with future work requirements. But it is not uncommon for placement students to have quieter periods – at these times, both you and your manager will find access to previously identified and prioritised learning as a very effective alternative use of your time.

8.9 Reflective learning

There is no fixed format for reflective learning – what is more important is that you step back critically and review how you have performed a piece of work, and that you then understand what you could do differently next time. Some students (and managers) do not find this straightforward, so this short example below shows the type of reflection you might include in your learning journal. Note that it:

- Is relatively short.

- *Reviews* what went well, and not so well.

- *Plans* what you would do next time.

- Plans further learning.

- Includes how you felt at the time.

Example of reflective learning for Learning Journal

Introduction

- I was asked to prepare the monthly sales figures for the region, and present them to the next team meeting, with recommendations about what we need to do in the next quarter.
- This was a rush job, since the usual sales co-ordinator had been on a course, then went on holiday, so I only had four days to discuss what was usually done.

What went well

- The presentation on the day went well, and my manager thanked me for filling in at short notice.
- Most of the figures were ready on time.
- I was able to show the figures graphically, which doesn't seem to have been done before, which seems strange.

What didn't go so well

- One of the sellers said that the figures didn't look right, and that a big sales order completed half a day before the cut off hadn't appeared in the figures.
- I didn't understand two sets of abbreviations, which was a bit embarrassing when I was asked what they meant.

How I would do things differently next time

- The sales administration office didn't have the figures ready on the day they were supposed to, so I had to work at home to get these ready – somebody then said this always happens. So next time I

---

will tell them clearly when I need the figures, and check with the supervisor a couple of days earlier if they are likely to be late.
- I will learn the abbreviations in advance!
- I didn't understand the point about late figures, so I will double check with the sales supervisor if all work has been processed, and show on the graph the actual cut-off time.

Further Learning?

- I know I sounded nervous when I presented the figures, but I used the presentation techniques we had been taught, and at least they followed what I was saying. Next time, I know that I can be more confident – I did OK this time, and know now how to get the figures right in advance – I feel good about this.

8.10 Mentors

Finding a mentor

When you start in your host organisation, you may be offered a mentor. The role of the mentor is to provide a more independent third party, who can advise you, discuss your progress, and take a wider view than may be possible with your line manager, or a learning and development adviser within the HR department. They can then help you to set up your own action plan, having been able to discuss the issues with an 'independent' adviser.

If you are offered a mentor, the ways of working together will normally be explained to you. Mentors may be trained in their role (for example, at BP), or at least have formal guidance about their role. Your mentor may suggest a formal meeting schedule (for example, meeting once a month), or may simply offer to be there when needed.

Mentors do this work in addition to their normal work roles, and you will get as much from the mentoring relationship as you put into it. For example, when you have a meeting booked with your mentor, think about what you want to get from the meeting in advance. Good practice is to do a short note (maximum one page) on what you have been doing, and what you want to get from the meeting: send this to your mentor about four to five working days ahead of your scheduled meeting date.

If your host organisation does not even have an informal mentor scheme, still consider having a mentor to help you navigate your way through your placement (and, as you will find, your later career too). Discuss this with your manager or any placement student who has recently worked in the organisation. Your mentor may be outside your host organisation – the important thing is that you can get on with each other, respect each other's views, even if these may be different, and have the willingness to make the mentoring relationship successful.

If you have a mentor, you are likely to develop broader perspectives than if you only rely on the direction and support of your line manager, valuable as this may be. Should you find yourself with difficult decisions or situations, your mentor's greater experience may help you to navigate your way through. And just sometimes, mentors' broader perspectives can help you to develop your network of contacts and possible longer term job opportunities.

To find a mentor, ask your manager for a recommendation, and approach that person to see if he/she would be willing to work with you on this basis. Some organisations may already have a list of people who have offered to be mentors, thus making your initial approach that much easier. Explain what you hope to get from the mentoring relationship, and how often you would like to meet. Agree with your mentor a meeting schedule, and check two to three days in advance that it is still convenient for your mentor that you should meet. When you see your mentor, it is possible that they will appear to take the lead by asking you how things are progressing.

Use your time with your mentor effectively. Prepare for the meeting in advance by having a short agenda, and notes relevant to the meeting. You should be able to discuss anything with your mentor, in confidence. However, topics which you may find it helpful to discuss with your mentor to establish a business-like relationship could include:

- Preparation and progress for work, a presentation, or a project with which you are involved.

- Review/reflection on how a work assignment or project has gone.

- Where you may have difficulty navigating your way through organisational structures, or politics.

- Advice on the type of future assignment or learning which would be beneficial in extending your learning.

Why placement students need mentors
(In conversation with Professor David Clutterbuck, author of *Everyone Needs a Mentor*, 2004)

The value of placement students having a mentor

Having a mentor provides people arriving in a new environment with a powerful resource for understanding the culture they have entered. It gives them an empathetic colleague, to whom they can turn when they feel uncertain or unvalued (particularly common when the placement organisation hasn't really prepared for receiving them). Self-esteem tends to be higher amongst placement students, who have an effective mentor.

The value of managers having students as mentees

All teams gravitate towards groupthink as the members become familiar with each other's ways of thinking. The placement mentee, properly used, can provide a level of naïve challenge to what the team does and how it does it.

The most common benefit expressed by effective mentors is the challenge they receive from their discussions with their mentee. Where there is a generation gap, the value of this challenge is greatly increased.

As a student, the particular things you need to develop in mentoring relationships are:

- Make clear your own learning needs.
- Ask the mentor about the learning they would like to gain from the relationship.
- Balance listening, questioning and challenging what you see and hear.
- Show that you value the attention you receive from them.
- Always prepare for mentoring sessions (What do I want to discuss? What examples can I use? etc.).
- Always spend time afterwards reflecting on what you have learned from the mentoring conversation and how you can apply this learning.
- Have in mind the potential for you to become a mentor in due course: what can you observe from this mentoring relationship that will build on your own mentoring skills?

8.11 Networking

Why network

It's true! Effective networking really can open up new opportunities for you. Some of the advantages of effective networking are:

- Organisation awareness: a better understanding of the structure and functions of the organisation, who does what and where, and organisational politics.

- Movement of people: as you broaden your networks, you will gain a better understanding of how and where job opportunities are created. Understand how people from one area are considered for work in other areas, or, alternatively, if there are job moves which do not seem to happen – why not?

- Job or training opportunities inside or outside the organisation.

- You never know what may turn up!

How to network

Networking is widely accepted in organisations. But being obvious about it is regarded as being over-instrumental, and is usually a major turn-off for most people. So it is important to make and take good opportunities to network in an acceptable way.

You can network at formal events, such as courses and team briefings, as well as less formal events – perhaps leaving drinks for a colleague – and even less formal occasions, such as waiting for lunch, at the coffee machine, etc.

The important thing is how you network. And key to this is showing interest in the other person, rather than seeking to impress the other person. Here are some ideas for good networking:

- As a general rule, quality of network contacts is far more important than how many people you try to network with.

- Be aware that networking can happen at any time. Be ready for it.

- Show an interest in the other person, by asking questions: Where do you work? What do you do? Quickly move beyond questions which have yes/ no, or single word answers – they are unlikely to engage a conversation, and, at worst, can sound as though you are putting the other person through the third degree. So more open questions (such as 'What do you think of...?', or 'How do you find...?') are much more likely to nurture a net-worked relationship.

- Offer help or information as easily as you may seek it, since this is far more likely to establish trust in a relationship.

- When you are talking to one person, maintain interest and eye contact. There is little worse than a forced conversation with one or both of you scanning the room for somebody more interesting to speak to.

- Follow up afterwards, if appropriate. If you have said that you would send an article or some information, make sure that you do so promptly.

- Finally, networking is about making sense of random connections. The person who is not obviously a useful network connection may be one step away from a contact that will be. So this is also a reminder: networking is of value, but only really works when we treat people as though they are also valued, and are not just a means to an end.

8.12 Leadership and management

If you plan to be a manager yourself during your career, your placement will be a good opportunity to:

- See and experience at first hand the differences and similarities between good leadership, and good management.

- Develop a deeper understanding of the similarities and differences between leadership and management.

- Work out your preferred style, and how you will become effective in these critical roles.

So far, we have considered how to be effective in an organisation by looking at the competences and behaviours which are most likely to make you effective (so, delivering results, team working, and so on). As we discuss leadership and management, we will look at what leaders and managers actually do.

Social scientists have found it difficult to say what the elements of good leadership are. If you think about leadership across history, that difficultly becomes apparent, especially as characteristics of good leadership in one situation (for example, war) may be quite different from those required at key times of social or national change. So, whatever you may think about the values of leaders such as Napoleon, Churchill, Geldof, or Mandela, all had different things to achieve in the leadership they gave to people at a particular time, and in their styles of achieving this. But the one thing that we can say about these and other leaders is that they had a clear sense of focus – of what needed to be done – and how they wanted to do it. As with other leaders, they had a firm view of what they wanted to do, the process they would adopt to do this, and that this was the right action at the time to enable large numbers of people to share a new vision, and engage and work to a new direction, by feeling inspired and motivated by that leader to do so.

Good management is different from good leadership, but there are overlapping elements in both activities. Managers are more likely to be involved in the technicalities of the job to be done (such as planning and resource allocation), but will also have wider roles akin to leadership, such as acting as a figurehead to the team, and communicating with the team and others.

One of the classic views of the role of the manager is presented by Mintzberg (1975), who suggested that managers have some or all of the following roles:

1 *Figurehead*: as a representative of the organisation.

2 *Leader*: interacts, motivates, develops team members.

3 *Liaison*: networks with contacts inside the organisation, and through professional bodies.

4 *Monitor*: gathers information from within and outside the organisation.

5 *Disseminator*: communicates information to the team on a group or one to one basis.

6 *Spokesperson*: provides information to people outside the organisation.

7 *Entrepreneur*: designs and initiates change in the organisation, which may include working hours, new ways of working with processes, products, or technology.

8 *Disturbance handler*: deals with problems as they arise.

9 *Resource allocator*: controls people, budgets, resources, allocation of time, etc.

10 *Negotiator*.

Mintzberg's role of the manager is written in terms which may be different from today's competence language, and some of the roles indicative of a manager may also be performed by employees who are not managers themselves. Nevertheless, Mintzberg's list gives you a useful benchmark to consider those activities you may expect to see in managers, and how these are being performed.

So back in your placement, which styles work well in the way supervisors and managers work with people, and which do not work well, and why? Are there differences between short-term and long-term styles? What works, and what leaves you and your colleagues motivated, keen to learn, and productive and effective? What doesn't work and leaves you ineffective, exasperated, and stressed? Why do these things happen in these ways, and are there alternative approaches which could be used? What additional factors would you add to Mintzberg's list? For example, how important is the technical capability to perform the role? Is Mintzberg's list too passive for the twenty-first century – for example, should 'delivering results' be part of a manager's role? Are some aspects of a manager's role so fundamentally important that they should be mentioned as an additional role, such as developing a diverse and balanced team, without a bias according to gender, ethnicity, disability, age, or orientation and beliefs?

If you are aspiring to be a future manager this is also a good time to think about your own personal styles, why you would chose those approaches, and what strengths and development areas you have; you should note these in your personal development plan.

8.13 Continued Professional Development (CPD)

If, after your degree result and graduation, you plan to join a professional body, you may be able to have part of your work placement count towards your CPD for membership. Check on the membership site to see what your professional requirements are, whether pre-registration is required, and what format is necessary for any record keeping and learning logs.

8.14 Summary

What distinguishes your learning in an organisation from your university learning is the much greater emphasis which organisational learning places on learning by doing. But just doing is not sufficient for you to learn – it must be linked to a methodical approach, clear personal objectives, and an understanding of what you personally find most – and least – comfortable in your personal learning styles.

8.15 Further information

Further reading

Clutterbuck, D. (2004) *Everyone Needs a Mentor*. London: CIPD.
The leading book for mentors and those seeking a mentor – how to get one, and how to manage the relationship effectively.

Furnham, A. (2005) *The Psychology of Behaviour at Work*. Hove and New York: Psychology Press.
For an excellent discussion about characteristics, roles, and styles of leadership and management, and a consideration of a wide and interesting account of peoples' behaviour in the workplace.

Green, F. (2006) *Demanding Work*. Princeton: Princeton University Press.
Written by an economist, this takes a tough look at how and whether factors such as the growing affluence and the knowledge economy really make a difference to our quality of working life.

Honey, P. and Mumford, A. (2006) *The Learning Styles Questionnaire, 80 Item Version*. Hastings: Peter Honey.
Questionnaire to find out what your preferred learning styles are likely to be.

Professional bodies

If you are preparing your career for a particular profession, check their websites for up to date information on the following.

What issues/topics are currently important? Include them on your learning objectives. CPD requirements: What are they? Can you register now? Will your placement count towards CPD?

Having followed up on your CPD, make sure you do CPD as you go along – don't leave it to the end of your placement.

Checklist

1 Check your learning style, and understand the strengths you may achieve and the development opportunities which you may miss with this style.
2 Get yourself a learning journal; if you cannot trust yourself to update this as events happen, diarise to update your journal at a given time, for about 30 minutes, every week.

(Cont'd)

---

3 Find one or two mentors – work out when and how often it is most
   productive to meet; make sure you are properly prepared before
   you go to see your mentor.
4 Look widely to develop your learning – what people do in their
   work is important, and you need to understand and perform well
   in what you do and how you do it. But look more broadly than
   this – how and why do they work in this way? How might it
   be done differently (and why isn't it done differently)? What
   influences do individual and team behaviours have on the way
   work is done? How are people managed within the organisation?
   How do you prefer to be managed? What will be your preferred
   management style(s) and why?
5 Always scan the organisation for new learning opportunities during your placement – on the job training, volunteering for assignments, etc.
6 By the end of your placement, if you have managed your learning well, you will be able to explain it clearly because it is in
   your Personal Development Plan or your Learning Journal, and
   you will have kept these up to date as your placement progresses. If you leave this to the end of your placement, whether
   for university or professional CPD purposes, you will be tearing
   your hair out ... and you will have missed valuable learning in
   the process of your placement.

Section 3

University and Placement

Many students become deeply involved with the work at their placement organization – and it is right to give it your commitment and energy. But don't forget also that you are on the placement to learn, and you may have university work to complete as well. This may include a portfolio, report, or dissertation. So in this section, we share some practical advice about managing your university work during your placement.

Chapter 9

University Research Principles

Chapter contents

During your placement and internship, you have two priorities coming from two different organisations: impressing your work-based organisation with your skills, and sustaining your university course work. So far we have emphasised the organisation, but now we turn our attention to getting that university work done on time, and to a high standard.

This chapter is intended to give you practical advice on how to navigate your way through your dissertation. It is not intended as a substitute for more intensive preparation and reading on research methods, and ideas for additional reading are given at the end of the chapter.

9.1 Organising for success

As important as it is to make a good impression with your placement organisation you will probably have a major piece of university work to complete as well. Usually, though not always, this will be a dissertation or extended management report. This is likely to have a major impact on your final degree classification, so it is important to get it right. As with all things in your degree course, the time for preparing for this work, and actually undertaking it, will come very quickly.

Managing your dissertation is your key work priority, so do not be deflected by being 'too busy at work' to give it the attention it requires. It is easier to explain to a future employer how you got a good degree during your placement, than how you took on too much work and suffered with your final degree result. This is a key time to develop the way you manage competing priorities, so plan this carefully.

Your placement dissertation is likely to be the longest piece of work you will have to undertake to date. With good planning, it will be a rewarding and interesting experience.

Whilst the technicalities of your dissertation may cause some challenges, your supervisor will be able to help you with those aspects you have not worked through yourself. But the most common reason for dissertation stress is mismanaging time: what seems a long time at the start to read, research, and write your dissertation, fades away very quickly. You should expect that each stage will take two to three times longer than you may reasonably expect, and preparation times (for example, for in-company research) will always take longer to write, test, and get signed off than you may expect.

9.2 Working with your tutor

It is very important that you establish and maintain an effective working relationship with your dissertation supervisor. Part of the responsibility for doing this is, of course, lies with your supervisor, but you will also have an important role in making sure this works well. As with your host organisation manager, your supervisor will probably have a high and diverse workload, and may be supervising several students at the same time. So, you will benefit most if you can make the working relationship cordial but also efficient.

Be very clear about your university's dissertation requirements, including hand-in dates, length, presentation format, and any interim reports which need to be submitted. Find a diary or year planner which covers the period of your placement and dissertation, and make a note of these key milestone dates now.

Agree a work programme with your supervisor, and also agree how you will schedule meetings during this period. Make a note of those dates on your work planner, and plan to ensure that you will have suitable material to send to your supervisor in advance of your meeting dates.

When you meet with your supervisor, do listen carefully to their advice and guidance. This may be easier advice to read than it is to follow. Your supervisor probably does not know your host organisation as well as you do, and you need to have independence in your own thoughts and approaches. If you are not clear what your supervisor means, then ask further questions. Aim to leave your supervisory meetings with new insights, and a refreshed enthusiasm for your assignment.

It is good practice to write up a page of notes and actions soon after your supervisory meeting; your supervisor may also find it useful to have a copy of these notes.

9.3 Research topic

Your placement organisation or your university may already have a topic for your research dissertation, or be willing to leave this to you. You may be tempted to think that your own choice of dissertation topic is the easier route, but if you have been told what you need to research, you will at least know that the organisation or your university is interested, committed, or prepared for this research, so time spent on you thinking about what to do, and then gaining acceptance, is reduced.

However, if you do have the opportunity to choose your own topic, here are some of the factors you should consider with your host organisation manager and your university tutor:

- How and why is the topic relevant to the organisation?

- How and why is the topic of wider interest?

- Am I genuinely interested in this area, and prepared to be immersed in it?

- What work have I previously done in this area which validates my choice?

- What literature is available in this area? What are the areas of controversy which may be worth exploring further (at this stage, you will have outline ideas only, and will develop them later)?

- Are your ideas on how you would undertake organisational research in this area practical (discuss with your manager)?

- Who are the key stakeholders within the organisation who will be interested in this research?

Common mistakes

Selecting a dissertation topic

- Making the terms of reference too wide – it is better to analyse your topic in depth, rather than have a wide ranged topic, which you can analyse in shallow terms only.
- Unrealistic timelines – your literature research, organisation research, and writing up are likely to take much longer than you expect, so plan accordingly.
- Failing to get your organisation's approval in sufficient time.
- Failing to clear ethical considerations (for example, university, organisation, especially in the NHS).

(Cont'd)

Field research

- Failing to plan sufficient time in advance … it will take much longer than you think to plan, get returns, arrange to meet people, etc.
- Failing to think through an appropriate research approach (qualitative, quantitative, or a mixture of both).
- Progressing a research approach without doing a short pilot study first to test reliability and practicality.
- Failing to get clearance from all relevant stakeholders for your research.
- Planning to finish your research after you have left the organisation. It is much easier for you to plan and complete this, and for your placement colleagues to co-operate, when you are still in the organisation.

Structure

- Failing to ensure that the structure of your paper appears as a 'joined up' piece of work. To avoid this, ensure that your literature review, research methods, and research findings link together as one document, and are not separate and fragmented chapters. Key to doing this well is to be sure that your research question is clear, and that your literature review is well structured. It should then be possible to frame your research findings within similar headings to the literature review, so that the paper is easier to read, and you can easily discuss and cross reference your findings to the literature headings.

Writing

- Telling yourself you can't 'get into it' to start writing … just start!
- Telling yourself that you always work best to short deadlines … this is a much bigger piece of work so do start early!
- Failing to check your work thoroughly.
- Over-reliance on computer-based spell checking to edit for you (it will let through correctly spelt but wrong words).

9.4 Research approaches

The classic approaches to research are to use quantitative and qualitative methods. It is not intended here to consider the academic advantages and disadvantages of each approach, but there are some practicalities which you should consider, and these are set out in Tables 9.1 and 9.2.

Table 9.1   Advantages and disadvantages of qualitative research survey methods (usually face-to-face, for example, focus groups, 1:1 interviews)

Advantages	Disadvantages
Can give an understanding of *how* and *why* people feel as they do	Results are particular to the individual employees included in the research, and difficult to generalise for wider populations
	Results may appear to be more complex to interpret than for quantitative research
Better understanding of *how* and *why* people feel as they do assists more focused management actions to follow up from surveys	May be difficult to summarise and benchmark findings, from one time period to another, or from one team to another
Especially valuable when addressing a detailed understanding of how and why people feel as they do	Employees may believe they are less likely to be anonymous, so will need clear undertakings and safeguards
Discursive nature of this research means employees are less inclined to take tactical or careless positions with answers to survey questions	Can be more time consuming than quantitative research
Discursive nature of this research helps to underpin the research subject view that researchers are listening and interested in their views	Researchers need the time and skill to lead meaningful 1:1 or focus group meetings
	If focus groups are used, this requires good facilitation skills to avoid 'group think'

Table 9.2   Advantages and disadvantages of quantitative research survey methods (usually completing a questionnaire, for example, paper-based or web-based)

Advantages	Disadvantages
Can survey total population	Not all may respond, so results can be distorted and may not be fully generalisable statistically
Answers to questions can be presented as metrics	Metrics themselves may require a deeper investigation to understand *why* people think as they do
Can be undertaken with only basic statistical knowledge ...	... but not too basic! Make sure you have a clear idea of how you will use statistical analysis and agree this with your supervisor

(Cont'd)

Table 9.2

Advantages	Disadvantages
Metrics tell us what people think	Metrics may not tell us how people actually behave (also applies to qualitative research)
Provides an accessible basis for follow-up qualitative research	Questions must be unambiguous
Questionnaires can be undertaken anonymously, so encouraging participation	Respondents may try to 'vote' tactically to achieve particular outcomes
The number and phrasing of questions must be managed with care	Too many questions may lead to a tick box mentality from respondents

Arnold, J (1997) Managing Careers into the 21st Century, Paul Chapman Publishing Ltd. London

Comment: Full details retained so can go straight to your own bibliography

Main Library, 658.301ARN

Comment: Which library book obtained from, and reference retained, just in case of need to refer to again

Overall: useful book with many different career perspectives

Comment: Short note on how useful you thought the book would be

P16 career definition 'A career is a sequence of employment-related positions, responsibilities, role, activities and experiences encountered by a person'

Comment: Example of a quote from the book which you might use in your own literature review

P25 UK Labour Force prediction 2006

Comment: Statistics reminder – may need to get more up to date figures

Etc etc

Comment: Notes can build up for direct and referenced quotes, other sources referred to, critique, etc.

Figure 9.1   **Sample of record keeping for literature review**

9.5 Literature research

The literature research is critical for your dissertation. The literature section:

- Sets out the theory for your paper.
- Gives you the chance to show that you understand that theory, and can balance this with critical evaluation.
- Relates your research findings back to the literature and any previous research findings.

You will be handling a much higher volume of literature than for previous work you have completed, and good organisation is essential. Bespoke software (e.g. Refworks or End Notes) may be available to help to organise your bibliography. However, good note taking and record keeping are essential: keep notes so that when you have used a book or article you can return it having retained everything you need for your dissertation. These notes may be kept on a paper card system, journal, or on computer, and may look like those shown in Figure 9.1.

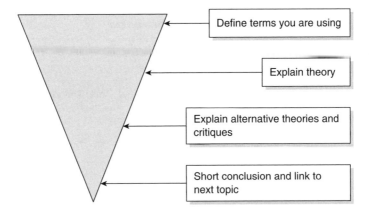

Figure 9.2   How a topic may be built up in the literature review

Provided that you have done sufficient research, the key to writing a good literature review is to use a clear structure, so that the reader has a clear idea of the definitions you are using, the theories supporting the topic and a critical evaluation of those theories. Each element of theory which you address in your literature review should be presented in a clear and well structured approach, as suggested in Figure 9.2.

The overall literature review may then be developed using areas of theory as building blocks for a clear and well structured review, as demonstrated in Figure 9.3.

9.6 Ten steps to managing your dissertation

Your workplace dissertation is a major project in its own right, and needs substantial planning. In this section we will discuss ten key steps in how you can go about this.

1   Reflect on your previous written assignments.

2   Be clear about your university requirements.

3   Establish a contact programme with your dissertations tutor, and stick to it.

4   Understand and respect all key stakeholder requirements.

5   Plan a realistic schedule.

6   Chose a topic which you will find interesting.

7   Observe ethical/professional standards for your university and host organisation.

8   Ensure a work/life balance.

9   Manage risks.

10   Keep to your writing schedule.

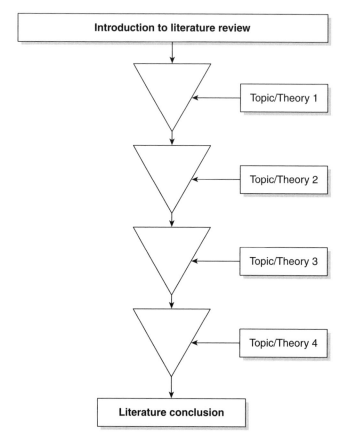

Figure 9.3   **How to build up areas of theory into a well structured and cohesive literature review**

Sample dissertation timeline

Set up a realistic timeline, diarise this on your year planner, and make sure you stick to the plan. If you have less time than this, scale your planning accordingly.

Agree dissertation topic with placement organisation and university supervisor.	Month 1
Start literature review.	Months 1–3
Scope research approach.	
Sign off research approach with organisation and university.	Months 2–3
Set up appointments for field research.	Month 3
Commence field research.	Month 4
Start writing.	Months 4–5
Finish.	Month 6

1   Reflect on your previous written assignments

Your dissertation will probably be the largest piece of research and writing you will have to undertake to date, and may be the largest piece of work that you do for some years in your career. So it is important that you think about it carefully, as you start detailed planning.

Think about any previous research and written work that you have done:

- Check back to papers you have previously written. What went well/not so well as you undertook the literature research?

- What feedback did you receive from your tutor on your writing style, and on the content of your paper?

- Are you clear about the layout requirements for your dissertation?

- Are you clear about how your university wants references to be shown? Have you consistently used correct referencing?

- Did you really understand the referencing requirements?

- Think about when you did a particularly good paper – how did you plan and manage your time throughout this process?

- Equally, think about a time when things may not have gone so well – how did you resolve this? How could you avoid similar challenges with your [longer] dissertation? How much time did you allow yourself to do this work, and how much time did you take? Did/do you allow yourself to procrastinate when writing? When and how does this happen? How will you reduce these risks with your dissertation? Where do you find that you are most productive in writing? What time of day are you most productive in your writing?

As you plan your dissertation writing, use this reflection checklist to consider how things have gone in the past. Then, based on this, start to make *realistic* plans for your dissertation.

2   Be clear about your university requirements

Following the university requirements in submitting your dissertation should be the easiest part of the dissertation, but this is often looked at only cursorily by some students, so causing unnecessary rework and stress.

- Your university will have a coursework dissertation handbook, so make good use of it.

- Ensure that you understand and follow university requirements on dissertation layout (the structure and order of your final paper) and presentation (including correct line spacing and print size).

- Don't make mistakes about referencing conventions – find and print the university referencing requirements, and keep them with your dissertation handbook.

- If your dissertation needs to be bound, remember to factor this into your workplan. Remember too, that if you plan to finish around the due date for your dissertation, so too will your fellow students, with a consequent pressure on the printing and binding shop. Early completion will reduce the risks of you handing in late because you couldn't get your work bound in time.

3 Establish a contact programme with your dissertations tutor, and stick to it

Your supervisor is likely to have a diverse portfolio of work to manage already, and also likely to have been allocated quite a limited time allowance to support and mark your dissertation. So it is important that you are proactive in finding time and space in your supervisor's diary for your work, and using that time effectively.

To do this:

- Your supervisor may set key milestone dates and meetings with you. If not, it is a good idea for you to ask to see your supervisor at agreed time intervals.

- Once you have a good idea of the time scales for your dissertation, suggest a series of meetings with your supervisor, and what you hope to achieve by each meeting date.

- Once you have set these dates, stick to them, and make sure that you engage your supervisor with written material/ideas in time for each meeting.

- Keep your dissertation supervisor periodically up to date – this may be for issues such as to tell your supervisor about key events in your placement, or to ask for brief advice about an issue in your research. Without pestering your supervisor, your aim is to maintain a steady and business-like contact, so that when you do see your supervisor, both of you can re-engage quickly with your research topic.

4 Understand and respect all key stakeholder requirements

Plan who are to be the key stakeholders in your research. Clearly, you, your placement organisation manager, your dissertation supervisor, and your university are important. But so are the following people also:

The people who you may be researching

It is possible that they have participated in research programmes previously, but for most research subjects, this will be their first time. They will be interested in the research, but may be anxious as well – for example, will they say the 'wrong things' to you? Will you disclose information which they have given in confidence to other people, especially their more senior managers? How will their privacy be protected?

You can allay many of these fears – and so obtain more honest feedback from interviews – by having a clear statement of research ethics at the start of your interviews. There are a number of guides on what you can and should do here, and these are listed at the end of this chapter.

As you write to confirm the arrangements for your research interviews, include a short statement on how you will ensure the confidentiality of your research interviews, for example, by using the wording in the following box.

Sample research confidentiality undertaking

Thank you for agreeing to participate in this research programme.

The research will be undertaken in accordance with the code of practice for ..., and I can provide you with a copy of this should you wish to see it. The data you provide me with will be recorded and analysed. The data may also be incorporated into further analysis as part of the final research report.

However, I assure you that no information will be published or shared with any other person in such a way that individuals are identifiable.

The people who may be providing you with information

Make sure that the people you ask for information understand why you are asking for it, and that you plan to use it for your dissertation. Check whether you may cite the information in your dissertation, and mention this as your source – it is helpful to do this in writing and to keep a record of the permission you have received.

Remember too that you will need to give adequate notice of your requests for information, and that you will also need to be very clear about the parameters of the information you are requesting. If possible, discuss the information request with the provider first – you may find that they have added comments and ideas which will help you.

5 Plan a realistic schedule

Schedule to complete your research fieldwork *before* you leave your placement organisation, and *after* you have already undertaken a significant amount of your literature review, even if you have not yet written this up.

Diarise when your dissertation is due for submission. If you have sufficient time, identify an earlier date, say three weeks before the hand-in date, when you plan to finish – this will build in a contingency period if something goes wrong. Now build a plan back from this date to do your dissertation.

6   Choose a topic which you will find interesting

This sounds so obvious! It may be that your placement organisation already knows what it would like to have researched. This spares you the anguish of thinking about what you might wish to study, but takes away some of your freedom as well. However, as long as you feel competent to tackle the proposed topic, then at least you can assume that the placement organisation has a need and management sponsorship to commit their time and resources to your area of study.

   However, if you have the freedom to choose your own area of study, here are some of the factors you may wish to consider:

- *Accessible literature*   Before finally committing yourself to a research area, spend a little time ensuring that you can get the books, journal articles, and other media which you will need. If you are away from university, can you access this remotely? Have you checked, and made sure, that journal search engines are as easily accessible and efficient remotely? Remember, too, to ensure that you have all the appropriate log-ins and journal passwords.

  If you think you may want to use university library facilities near your place of work, or home (if these are away from your university location), you may be able to do so using the SCONUL scheme. For details, see http://www.access.sconul.ac.uk or enquire at your university library.

- *Organisational commitment to your chosen topic*   Try to select a topic that is also of interest to your placement organisation. The more interested your placement organisation is, the more likely they will be to give you time and access to the people and information to support your research.

- *Sense of what your contribution will be*   If the research topic has ticked all the right boxes so far – you have access to good literature sources, the organisation is interested, you have an idea of how you might research it – then the final check is to ask yourself what contribution you may make to the area? This does not have to be detailed. It will almost certainly change and adapt during the research process, and it would be pointless to research a topic if you already 'knew' the answer! But having a sense of what you expect to find, and how you would use it, is important and will help as you shape your literature review, research approach, and discussions with your tutor.

7   Observe ethical/professional standards for your university and host organisation

It can be too easy to think about your research as a task to undertake and as data to be collected and written up. But your research is unlikely to be of any real value unless it finds new information, insight, processes, or meaning. And to do this, it is likely to be intrusive into individuals' personal details or opinions. Any inappropriate release of this information may cause embarrassment or worse for the individuals you are researching. If the research is intrusive into their personal views, your questions may also cause personal distress and you might not even be aware of this.

For this reason, many professional bodies, universities, and some organisations (for example, the NHS) have strict ethical and/or professional standards which you must comply with. Your university is most likely to give you direction on ethics, but do check with the professional body for your discipline (see the list at the end of this chapter) and also your host organisation manager.

8 Ensure a work/life balance

Your dissertation research and writing are important, but need to be managed with attention to your personal wellbeing. So, as you plan your schedule, make sure you also plan a life too! A longer dissertation timeline will ensure a better work/life balance than a short timeline, and will also probably enhance the quality of your dissertation as well. But think about your daily writing schedule too, and allow time for breaks and exercise.

9 Manage risks

Ensure that you think through what might go wrong in writing your dissertation and plan around this. The most common threats to completing a good dissertation on time are as follows.

Failing to plan for contingencies in your timescales

Don't expect that things will not go wrong – in view of the long time scales here, things are likely to go wrong at some point, so build in plans and extra time for this. It may be delays in getting your research done, an IT failure, difficulty in getting hold of literature, ill health, etc. Don't forget that these are contingencies periods, so do not use them to cushion for the fact that you may not feel like working, or have other priorities.

Failing to work effectively with your dissertation supervisor

Supervisors may be highly committed to helping you complete a great dissertation, or believe that it is up to you to take the initiative. Whichever, it is important that you establish an effective and business-like relationship with your supervisor.

At the conclusion of every meeting with your supervisor, write notes on what you have discussed, and what was agreed. Avoid feeling inhibited in what you discuss with your supervisor, or in showing early drafts of your written material – whatever you show your supervisor, it is unlikely to be the best or worst work which that supervisor will have seen. Supervisors well understand the challenges of researching and writing up material, and can only provide real help to you if you submit written work for them to review and comment upon, at the time you said you would submit that work.

If, having stuck to agreed meeting and writing schedules, you find that you cannot connect with your supervisor, then you must first discuss it with that person. This may help to clear up any miscommunication between the two of you. If it does not, then you may wish to ask the university to reassign you to a different supervisor.

Problems with research ethics or practicalities

Ensure that you reduce the risk of these problems by discussing them at the start of your dissertation with your dissertation supervisor at university, and with your manager in your placement organisation.

Your university supervisor will be able to tell you whether specific ethical approval is required, and guide you on the suitability and acceptability of your chosen research methodology.

Your placement organisation manager will be able to help you ensure that your research plans are achievable in the time frames you have planned, whether you will need specific organisational approval for your study, and that you manage organisational culture and politics and cultures appropriately, as well as the likely challenges you may face.

Losing research papers or written work

From the earliest stage in your writing, get into the habit of backing up everything in triplicate – just because you develop a paranoia about losing material does not mean that you will not lose it! For example, you may do this by always backing up on your computer's hard drive; using a dedicated memory stick for your dissertation; and by emailing to yourself the latest version (appropriately file referenced by the date or version number).

Students with disabilities

If you have a disability that may influence your ability to deliver your dissertation, make sure that your university is aware of it in advance, and has recorded it. The challenges of writing a good dissertation are sufficient in themselves, without added complications of late registration or failing to register relevant disabilities.

10   Keep to your writing schedule

For many students, writing up their research project is the most challenging part of the dissertation, and many more experienced writers would say that it doesn't get much easier. So good self-planning and self-discipline are essential.

Becker (1986: 149) suggests these straightforward steps:

1   Write with authority

2   Use a direct style of english.

3   Be prepared to edit at several different stages.

4   Be professional and make writing [or reading] an everyday occurrence.

5   Confront yourself with the risks of writing by allowing others to read your drafts.

6   Keep to deadlines however difficult it may seem.

From your reflection on your previous writing, you should have a good idea about what works well and not so well for you personally. But remember also with your dissertation that you will be dealing with higher volumes of written material than you may have produced in the past. You can help your writing schedule if you:

- Find a time in the day when you know that you are better at writing/working. If your energy levels are low at certain times of the day, there is no point planning to write at those times.

- Try not to finish a writing phase, having used up all your work and ideas to that point – leave a little writing for when you return, and that way you will find it easier to start writing again (in this case, finishing off) than if you have to start completely afresh with a new topic.

- Do not convince yourself that you have 'writers' block', or that you are too busy to start writing. You are not too busy – this is your dissertation we are talking about and, usually, a major part of your final assessment. Little is more important during the writing phase than getting your dissertation handed in in the time scales you have set yourself. If you do have 'writers' block' you may have not done enough research, or preparation, but more likely, you are avoiding getting started. And if you are 'too busy' at work, or with other activities, you need to step back and re-evaluate what are the really critical deliverables in your life at this important time.

- Try to plan your writing over a period, and not cram it into a short time frame. This way, you will be able to cover unexpected contingencies (for example, illness, domestic issues, loss of computer facilities, etc.). Furthermore, your ideas are likely to develop better if you allow yourself time to write and, when not actually writing, to allow your ideas to develop further as well.

- Allow yourself to write in short bursts, as well as setting aside longer periods in a day for writing. By sticking to a writing schedule of even short periods in a day, your writing will build up quickly, allowing you time to review and edit what you have prepared. Many people assume that you need at least two hours to 'get into the subject, and write about it'. However, recent research by Rowena Murray (2008) of Strathclyde University suggests that writing in short bursts of even half an hour can be very productive. Murray cautions against procrastination and the desire to find more time and more ideas to write, and says:

People have to be adaptable to how they write. You can use both snacks [short writing periods] and binges [long writing periods]. There may be fallow or low-output periods.

A third strategy proposed by Murray is 'writing retreats', where groups of writers, who may not even be writing about the same topics or from the same disciplines, will spend two to five days away from day-to-day interruptions, and focus on writing. This idea needs careful evaluation to ensure that any away time is spent productively; however, it may be especially helpful if you are completing your dissertation on a group basis. *If you work with others on your dissertation, remember that unless your work-based assignment is intended as a group project, the work which you submit must be your own, otherwise you may be accused of plagiarism.*

- Your dissertation will often be a major component of your final mark, and it is essential that you plan it properly. In many cases, you will have longer time scales for completion than for other assessed elements of your course. Use this time effectively, so that you do not have a log jam of assessment work in your final months of study. It is important that you allow sufficient time for all your assessed study, and that you do not allow the dissertation to dominate your time, at the expense of other course work, or vice versa.

- Before submitting your written submissions, make sure that you edit these very carefully. As a rule of thumb, a well written dissertation should be comprehensible to a lay person, even if some of the technicalities are not obvious. Ask a reliable friend to read it on your behalf, and to comment critically on it. Check spelling, referencing, and grammar very carefully. Do not over-rely on computer spell checks to do this for you, since they can often allow words to pass which are actually inappropriate in your text, for example, allowing 'form' when you meant 'from', or 'trial', when you meant 'trail'.

Writing your dissertation is a very important completion of your studies. At times it will be a frustrating, tiring, and perhaps worrying experience. But by using the tips discussed in this chapter, it can be a very rewarding experience. It will draw together your studies, and give you confidence that you can tackle similar large-scale projects in the future.

Good writing tips

- Plan time for writing, and stick to it.
- Accept that some periods of writing will be highly productive ... and other times you will write very little or feel that you are going backwards.

- Write first, edit later.
- Using a literature source? Put it into your bibliography *now*, not later; this will save time-consuming proof reading.
- Use a strong structure.
- Every little helps! Do not expect to be able to write pages every day. If your writing schedule says that you are writing that day, do something – even 300–500 words will keep your progress maintained and your thoughts focused.
- Reward yourself! With paragraphs or sections written, have a drink, or a short walk.

9.7 Further information

Useful further reading

Baxter, L., Hughes, C., and Tight, M. (2001) *How to Research*. Buckingham: Open University Press.
Good start-to-finish guide to choosing your topic, reading, research approaches, and writing up.

Becker, H. (1986) *Writing for Social Scientists*. Chicago: University of Chicago Press. (Cited in Easterby-Smith, M., Thorpe, R., and Lowe, A. (2003) *Management Research: An Introduction*. London: SAGE.)

Easterby-Smith, M., Thorpe, R., and Lowe, A. (2003) *Management Research: An Introduction*. London: SAGE.
Good book on approaches to research.

Gill, J., and Johnson, P. (1991) *Research Methods for Managers*. London: Paul Chapman.
Helpful guide on how to start the research process, and various approaches you can use.

Hart, C. (2001) *On Doing a Literature Review*. London: SAGE.
Excellent source book; written for social scientists, but with wider appeal; how to find and write up your literature search.

Saunders, M., Lewis, P., and Thornhill, A. (2003) *Research Methods for Business Students*. Essex: Pearson.

Walliman, N. (2008) *Your Undergraduate Dissertation*. London: SAGE.
An excellent and straightforward guide to planning and writing your dissertation.

Research codes of practice and ethics

Your university may have its own arrangements for the ethical approval of research, and you should ask your tutor about these. Some organisations, notably the National Health Service, have strict requirements for research approval, so you *must* also check these, even if the research is in a non-clinical/patient contact area.

In addition, professional bodies have research codes of practice, so do check these too. Some examples are listed below:

British Market Research Association   Code of Conduct at http://www.bmra.org.uk

The Council for Industry and Higher Education   Ethical Issues and Higher Education at http://www.cihe-uk.com/ethics.php

British Educational Research Association (BERA)   Ethical Guidelines at http://www.bera.ac.uk/guidelines.html

Health and Social Care

Research in the NHS – you must check with your NHS manager.

Central Office for Research Ethics Committees   http://www.corec.org.uk

Medical Research Council (MRC)   http://www.mrc.ac.uk/index/public_interest/public-ethics_and_best_practice.htm

Information Technology

British Computer Society (BCS)   http://www.bcs.org.uk/ethics/freedom.htm

Law

Socio-Legal Studies Association   http://www.ukc.ac.uk/slsa/download/ethics_drft.pdf

Politics

British International Studies Association (BISA)   http://www.bisa.ac.uk/code.htm

Psychology

British Psychological Society   http://www.bps.org.uk/documents/code.pdf

Sociology

British Sociological Association (BSA)   http://www.britsoc.org.uk/about/ethic.htm

Other general guidelines

Qualidata

Confidentiality and Informed Consent [Internet] http://www.esds.
ac.uk/qualidata/about/introduction.asp

Social Research Association http://www.the-sra.org.uk/index2.htm
http://www.the-sra.org.uk/ethics02.htm

Sociological Research Online http://www.socresonline.org.uk/info/ethguide.
html

Checklist

1 Make sure that you have a copy of your university's dissertation
   handbook.
2 Look over previous assignments you have written:

   Reflect on how these went well/not so well – how will you apply
   this experience to your dissertation?
   How effectively did you use reference protocols?

3 Check with your tutor and your manager what ethical or other
   approvals you will require in your dissertation.
4 As you read material for your dissertation, take full notes so that,
   in most cases, you can use these to write your dissertation and so
   do not need to take out the same books again.
5 Plan, realistically, how you propose to tackle your dissertation. Clear
   your plans with both your tutor and your in-company manager.
   Diarise these and stick to them.
6 Agree key milestones with your dissertation tutor, and arrange
   meetings in advance.
7 Never kid yourself that you are too busy for your dissertation – getting
   as much done as you can early on reduces the time your dissertation
   will clash with other work in your final year.

Section 4

Placements in Perspective

In this final chapter, three students discuss their own experiences of their placements. All three had successful placements – just as most students will have successful placement experiences. But there will still be areas which will go well and not so well, so think about their reflections on their experiences. Consider what they did well, and why, and what they wish they may have done differently.

Thinking about what you have learned from this book, how will you manage your own placement experience?

Placements are not just about getting a placement – hard as that might feel at times – nor are they about surviving – thriving – in the placement itself. Your placement is a means to an end: gaining employability skills; learning how to learn in the workplace; and understanding the interaction between university studies and organisational life. Returning to university needs a further adjustment and often right before your final assessment period. One student noted:

> It is hard to return to university – in terms of the work day not ending at 5 or 6 pm, but that you should be continuously working, even at weekends, as there is so much to do!! I think this was even more pronounced in the second placement as straight after this we went into the final year when it seems to get much harder!!

So far in this book, we have discussed practical ways to make the most of your placement. In preparing for this, do take the opportunity to speak to as wide a range of people as possible so as to get a better idea of what will be right for you. In this final chapter, we start those wider discussions with fellow students.

10.1 What makes a placement successful?

The short answer is ... you do.

Of course, there is more to it than this. Without a doubt, there are organisations which can be relied upon to offer an excellent placement experience and others which may offer the wrong roles, or the wrong individual manager to supervise the placement student. Similarly, universities may offer excellent or mediocre support to placement students.

But in the end much of the success of the placement rests with the individual student. For many, this represents a first encounter with really developing important skills for work and learning for the future – managing time effectively, balancing priorities, working with and influencing others, delivering results, and encountering and successfully navigating through problems on the way.

So whilst choosing a 'good' placement organisation helps to improve the chances of success, in the end it is your approach and personal organisation to the placement which will determine how successful it has been.

10.2 If you could do it all again …

Students interviewed as part of the research for this book were asked what they would have done differently, had they the chance to do it again. Here are their answers!

Top tips from students: what I'd have done differently

Before the placement

> Set myself clear objectives beforehand, then strive to achieve them.
> Prepared myself for drastic changes in lifestyle compared with university.
> Thought more about the type of organisation where I wanted my placement, and where it might lead to.
> Sent off more speculative applications.
> Prepared better: taken some time to understand the business first.

During the placement

> Discuss with your company what you want to get out of the placement.
> Got more sleep!
> Been more forward with some of my ideas; been more vocal on dull days.
> If it starts to go wrong, speak to your manager; don't ignore it, or be underhand.

10.3 Last words from universities

> ### Last words from universities
>
> - There is a placement out there for you – all you have to do is find it and make the most of it.
> - Try to see your academic work, your personal development, and your organisation work as 'joined up' topics – too many students look at them as being in separate and disconnected boxes.
> - Use this time of your life to gain 'out of the box' experiences.

10.4 Take three students

Student placement experiences vary considerably, but most students who undertake them enjoy them and learn from them. To give you some idea of what to expect, here are their accounts, in their own words, from students who have been through the process already.

As you read these accounts, think about your own placement as well … what you would have done similarly to these students, and what you may have done differently.

Paul

> ### Paul's placement experience
>
> *Decision to take a placement year*
>
> - Decided *after* starting university course.
> - Aiming for a better degree.
>
> *Finding a role*
>
> - Placement office.
> - Online applications to large organisations – found them slow getting back.
> - Smaller, local organisations better at replying.
>
> *(Cont'd)*

Induction

- Missed the general induction for placement students, but attended general talk, and Health and Safety briefing.

Benefits

- Training and work experience.
- Day trip to Toulouse!
- Working with a wide variety of senior managers.

Regrets

- None, though recognises less freedom.

Key learning points from Paul's placement

- Showed adjustment and resilience in workloads throughout placement – from not enough to do at first, then three separate managers, then given more senior work to do – all important learning opportunities.

Why did you choose to do a work placement?

When I started my course, I hadn't intended to do a placement ... I just wanted to do a three year course. But during my first year, I went to presentations on placements. They showed that you had a much better chance of a better job, and a better degree, if you did a year out. I am pleased with my decision to do a placement.

How did you conduct your job search?

I got my CV ready with help from the placement office, then did a lot of searches on the web, and with the placement office. I also did a lot of on-line applications to large organisations. They could be really bad at getting back to you: it's pretty upsetting at the time, because you spend a lot of time, even with online applications. When you get no response, no feedback, it's hard to know what you are doing wrong.

I also wrote by mail to local organisations, and sent out my CV. They were better at giving a response.

What were the most important factors for you?

I always wanted to go to a larger organisation. Location was also important: I wanted to stay near university if I could, or near home. I didn't want to be away from home and university.

When I came here, I had a very good impression of the organisation through my manager. In another organisation I applied to I knew I would be doing cold calling to customers to develop sales, and had real ethical problems about the way they worked.

Job title was pretty important, because I wanted a range of different activities.

Money wasn't a huge factor: I really wanted to look at the learning opportunities.

How were you assessed in your applications?

A range of interviews and assessment centres. In one placement I didn't get, I had interviews, did a presentation, and had a group discussion, I don't think I did very well, and hadn't had any practice in these areas. This taught me to be positive all the time in interviews and assessment centres, and to turn all the negatives into positives, by explaining what I had learned from different situations. In group discussions, I learned to listen to what others were saying in the team … not to jump in too quickly with my own views.

Tell me about your first week in your placement

I missed the main intake week, so I started later with five other interns. The first day was a lot of form filling, health and safety briefings, security passes, that sort of thing. There was also a talk from HR about making the most of the placement. In the first week, I met my colleagues and started work.

How is your work assessed?

It's very informal. I get feedback from my manager, but a lot of the work here is ad hoc. I only have specific objectives from the university.

What training have you received?

I have done Excel training courses on my own initiative, and the company has trained me on SAP.

What difficulties have you encountered?

At the start of my placement, I didn't really have enough to do, and seemed to spend a lot of time twiddling my thumbs. My manager tried to be helpful, but wasn't always there.

Then I had three different managers to report to. Prioritisation was important, but I felt that I had lots of competing demands, and couldn't do anything particularly well. It was stressful, and was resolved by allocating me to work for one manager only.

More recently, quite a few people have left, and I have effectively taken over a full-time role. I have been thrown in at the deep end, and have enjoyed that, but it can be quite hard too, for instance when you go to meetings without feeling that you are fully prepared.

What has given you the most satisfaction?

I have worked with a wide variety of people, and mixed with senior managers, so got to know how they think.

I have had a day trip to Toulouse. Financially, I have more money – I haven't saved anything, but I feel better off, and am no longer in debt.

Any regrets?

Not really. There is a lack of freedom.

How does a placement differ from university?

At university, you can work at any time, it's less structured, and your social life centres on your university friends.

On placements, you have a clear working day, which is both good and bad, but then you know that your work for the day is finished. You certainly have less freedom, and get tired more easily, so earlier to bed! I have learned how to work with people I probably wouldn't have worked with before. I have also learned how to dress properly for work ... and learned how to use an iron!

What about when you get back to university?

I will miss the variety and opportunities this placement have given me. I'll also miss the money. But I feel that I will be more committed to university life and making the most of my final year. I will be more structured and driven.

And now you are actually back at university ... ?

After I finished my placement, I was lucky enough to be invited to work as a subcontractor over the summer. I was also asked to work during my final year at university with the company but the demands of working two to three days a week as well as attending university were just too much.

Adjusting back to the university lifestyle was nice at first with more freedom and a few lay ins! The work schedule for the final year is however a lot more demanding – my year in the workplace has certainly stood me in good stead for this working long hours and managing my work with everything else in my life. I am also currently writing my dissertation and the information and insights I gained within the workplace have been key to my research findings.

I am now looking to apply for graduate schemes and am finding the application forms so much easier to fill in with all of the tasks that I have under my belt from my placement year.

How has your placement influenced your future career plans?

I do not want to be sat at a desk in front of a computer all day. I will want a role where I can meet people. It has given me a clearer impression of what I don't want to do: for example, finance!

Susan

Susan's placement experience

Decision to take a placement year

- Not sure about career plans – perhaps own business in due course.

Finding a role

- Online.
- Five applications overall, and invited to three assessment centres.

Benefits

- Excellent training, including developing IT and software skills.
- Wide variety of roles and experience.

Regrets

- None about the placement.
- But had been advised to keep a learning journal – didn't do so and now wishes she had.

Where now?

- Still not sure about long-term role, but more confident in tackling degree and finishing well.

Why did you choose to do a work placement?

I didn't know what I wanted to do when I left university. One day I might like to have my own business, but in the meantime, I thought that a placement would be good for my CV, and that the experience of working as part of my degree would be really important.

How did you conduct your job search? What were the most important factors for you?

A lot of web searches and using the university websites. I looked both at large and smaller organisations.

The most important factors were job title (I didn't want something too specific); variety of role; and a good organisation name. Then, money was important, though most of the salaries were pretty similar, to be near home or university, and the benefits of the role: I don't mind working hard, but some of my colleagues in placements in other organisations had really long working hours which I wanted to avoid.

How did you apply?

For all my applications, I applied online via the web, or by email with my CV. No post applications. I did five applications overall: I had three assessment centres, and accepted this role before my applications with two other employers had been finished.

How were you assessed in your applications?

For the three places I was shortlisted, I did interviews and assessment centres. The assessment centres included interviews, working in small groups, where we observed, and numeracy tests.

Tell me about your first week

On day one, we had an overall induction day with about 30 internships who started on the same day. On day two, I met the team I was to be working with, then met the rest of the people I was to be working with, and started working in the rest of the week. It was a bit scary at first, but I settled in happily. It will be a wrench to leave at the end of my placement.

How is your work assessed?

At the start of the year, I had my work objectives, personal objectives, and dissertation. My manager regularly helps me to understand my progress. I have a formal review and report mid year, and my placement officer visits to review my progress.

What training have you received?

Induction training, European Computer Driving Licence, SAP for HR and accounting. I also have on-the-job training and coaching. The previous intern had left a checklist for me, which was useful, and I will update that list for my successor.

What difficulties have you encountered?

I started by doing monthly management information returns. At first, the turnaround was three weeks, then two weeks, and now it is one week, so I had a lot of spare capacity once I got used to the work. When I need to find work to do, I speak to my manager. I've done some extra training, but then it gets hard to fill your day when there are only a few weeks left in your internship.

What has given you the most satisfaction?

The work is very varied, which is great. I find that it makes my university work much more relevant, so easier and more interesting to study. I am also lucky to be working in a great team.

Any regrets?

Not about my work, but we were encouraged to keep a learning journal by the university. I meant to start one, but I didn't. I wish I had kept a log of what I had done, and how my placement developed ... what I had achieved.

How does a placement differ from university?

Early starts! Obviously, you also have less freedom during the day, and less time to do other things. I find I am more tired ... in fact I am often shattered. The money is useful, though I don't feel that I am much better off financially.

What top tips would you pass on to other placement students?

Definitely do a placement. It will really boost your confidence and your capabilities.

It's really useful to have a mentor in the organisation ... my manager is also my mentor, and is a great support.

When you are on your placement, your work becomes much more structured – effectively, you are working all the time. I find this structure really useful, and know that I will apply the same routines when I go back to university.

Double check and review your work before you release it; make sure that it is fully correct. My attention to that kind of detail is still improving.

And how is it now that you are back at university?

I have always found my work experience in general a great advantage to my course before my placement, working in a retail shop and a pub restaurant.

My placement year enabled me to apply theory to practise further and to critique readings and theorists as I had a taste of a 'real job' especially as there was a great variety in my job role. I have also been looking for graduate jobs for when I finish my degree and finding my placement year has helped me narrow down my search into what I want to do and that a placement within your degree can help put you ahead of the competition!

How has your placement influenced your future career plans?

I am still not sure yet what I will do, but feel more confident about finishing my degree well, and that I know what I will be looking for in my career choice.

Leanne

Leanne's placement experience

Decision to take a placement year

- Had not intended to take a placement year, but attended presentations in first year and became convinced of value in experience, studying, and graduate career opportunities.

Finding a role

- Placement Office a great help.
- Applied to smaller and larger organisations – good success rate in being shortlisted.
- Some very positive job search experiences, and very negative experiences too.

(Cont'd)

Benefits

- Great training opportunities: eRoom training; and two days SAP training and events management training; health and safety training; trained as a recruitment assessor; e-learning media centre access for things like IT skills development.
- More confident with class participation.
- More confident with theory.

Regrets

- Only for a year!
- Don't get quite the same benefits and opportunities as graduate trainees.

Where now?

- Clearer sense of direction, rather than a clear-cut idea. Want to join a graduate trainee scheme for the good learning opportunities.

Key learning points from Leanne's placement

- Making and taking opportunities to undertake further training, develop and network once in a role.

Why did you choose to do a work placement?

I had no intention of doing a placement at the start of my course, but I changed my mind having attended university presentations about placements. I decided to do a placement so that I could put my studies into practice. I thought it would give a real-life application and I could see how things worked in practice. I also thought it would be good to find out more about the work environment, and I enjoy meeting new people and seeing new environments.

How did you conduct your job search?

The university was a great help as the Placements Office provided information on company websites, finding roles to apply for, CV preparation, and interview practice techniques.

I started looking early on in my second year, because I knew that a lot of the big companies filled their jobs early on. Smaller organisations in this area tended to fill their vacancies towards the end of the academic year in the spring and summer. Although I was offered interviews nearly everywhere I applied, I tried to learn from those times when I was rejected or not successful at interview.

What were the most important factors for you?

I wanted a good role, and where I am now sounded really good, and is good. I wanted to stay close to the university if I could, otherwise work in London or a large city.

I wanted a role that was fairly general and offered good opportunities for personal learning and growth.

Salary was less important, but I wanted to know that I would be paid fairly, and have enough to live on.

How did you apply?

For most jobs, I applied online. For smaller companies, I sent a covering letter with my CV; sometimes I telephoned them. Most places I applied to got back to me, but sometimes the time scales were really long, so I didn't always know what was going on.

How were you assessed in your applications?

Here, the selection process was simple and more informal: interviews, and meeting the managers. Elsewhere, there were interviews, presentations, that kind of thing.

Apart from this job, I was offered a job by a large international computer company. At the time, I turned it down because I didn't want to work in the location they had suggested, nor in the role. I explained this to them, and they were very good and suggested alternative roles elsewhere in the company, which impressed me. In another big international computer company, I did interviews, which I thought went well – but I never heard from them again– feedback would have been useful!

Tell me about your first week

The first half day was an induction which introduced the company, informed me about security, finding out where to park my car, then safety and security training. It was OK. I was then sent to find my department on this very large site, which was a bit scary. I then met the team, and the intern I was replacing then looked after me in the first week.

How is your work assessed?

I have a quarterly assessment from my placement office, which is just 'pass' or 'fail'. Here, I get feedback from managers and colleagues about my work. It is also great when they suggest 'Leanne would be good at that'.

For my dissertation, which is my next really big job, it is more difficult to tell how well I am doing at the moment.

What training have you received?

Quite a lot. I have done induction training; eRoom training; and two days SAP training and events management training. I have had health and safety training, and have been trained as a recruitment assessor. I also have access to the company's e-learning media centre for things like IT skills development, and the employee portal.

I have also done Myers-Briggs profiling, which has helped me to understand my personality and how I am likely to relate to others.

What difficulties have you encountered?

The placement has gone well, but I have encountered difficulties when school visits may not have gone so well, for example, when school visitors are noisey or ill-disciplined when visiting the site. It has taught me to make contingency plans, and to look for ways I can improve things.

What has given you the most satisfaction?

Everything! It has been great for networking, new friends, and new opportunities. I have attended conferences and exhibitions, schools and academies. As a result of my placement experience, I now expect to get a better class of degree.

Any regrets?

Yes, that it is only for a year. I suppose that we don't get quite the same benefits and opportunities as graduate trainees or full-time employees. But, really, there are very few disadvantages.

How does a placement differ from university?

As a student, you need to be much more self-motivated in your work. In a placement, life is much more structured, like getting up at 6 am and having a structured day ahead of you. I don't think there is so much difference financially; you still have to pay the rent, and other bills, though I am in less debt now.

I do also feel loyalty to this organisation, and I am proud to tell people who I work for.

What top tips would you pass on to other placement students?

Start your applications early, and don't give up. Even if you don't get a role by April, there are still jobs and you will get one if you try hard enough.

Make sure that your CV is as well written as it can be. Check your spelling is correct, make sure you give sufficient detail, and don't rush an application, because you can always tell if someone is just trying to justify themselves.

Be proactive in your placement, and volunteer for extra activities if you can.

How has your placement influenced your future career plans?

It has given me a clearer sense of direction, rather than a clear-cut idea. I definitely want to join a graduate trainee scheme as I have seen the good learning opportunities. Longer term, I may look at roles in resourcing or recruitment, or perhaps events management or project management.

Now you are back at university, has anything changed?

Going back to university is definitely different to the previous years. I am much more structured and get up early every day to get on with my work. I find I participate a lot more in seminars due to more confidence and a better understanding of organisations. Having done a placement also helps me reflect on theories and is useful to write about in my coursework. Overall I think I will achieve a better degree classification as a result of my experience.

10.5 Conclusion

Value of placements

As this book was being prepared, we met with a wide range of students, universities, and organisations involved with placements. The road to finding and settling in to a placement was not always easy. But everyone we spoke to reinforced the value they had gained in a placement. For the students, the experience had been beneficial and motivational in a personal growth in confidence, and a renewed vigour and personal organisation for their studies. Organisations had a variety of motivations for offering student placements – as additional support, as a way of developing learning in the organisation, to develop a recruitment pool for graduates, and even for more highly principled reasons such as developing the next generation of entrants with appropriate work skills. And for the universities too, the benefits could be seen in improved academic performance in the final year of studies, and greater employability skills and success.

Selection preparation

The range of possibilities and opportunities to find and benefit from a placement is extensive. Even after the research preparation for this study guide, it is obvious that we can only give a flavour of the types of placement opportunities available. However, a familiar message from many of the universities, organisations, and students and past students interviewed, is one of the value and potential value of placements. Sometimes this potential benefit is lost or diminished because of poor preparation for selection, or a failure to make the most of learning opportunities, or difficulty in coping with organisational processes and politics. By using this study guide effectively, we hope that you will avoid some of these pitfalls, and enjoy and make the most of your own placement experience.

Over to you!

We have finished this study guide with the stories of a small selection of placement students, who have agreed to share their experiences of the successes and occasional challenges of placements. We hope that their stories will help to inspire you, and that this book will also help you to navigate your way to a successful and fulfilling placement experience. Good luck!

(Post Placement) Checklist

1 Update your competence example table.
2 Ensure that your generic CV is fully up to date and includes new examples of your achievements during your placement.
3 Volunteer – to speak to the induction group for the next intake of students in your host organisation, or to potential placement students back at university.
4 Register your Continuing Professional Development papers with your future professional body if appropriate.
5 If you have a dissertation to finish writing, try to do as much of it as you can before returning to university, and certainly before Christmas of your final year – avoid getting your dissertation workload out of balance and damaging your marks in other subjects.
6 Stay in touch with your host organisation(s) – even a Christmas card will keep you on their radar for possible future opportunities, or will help smooth the path for future placement students.
7 Approach your studies, and your selection for graduate roles, with renewed energy, application and confidence – you have earned it!

Appendix

Useful Websites

AIESEC
AIESEC offers a wide range of international opportunities.
http://www.aiesec.org/cms/aiesec/AI/index.html

Directgov
For a wide range of information including tax and social security benefits.
www.direct.gov.uk/en/index.htm

GO Wales
Great selection of placements in Wales.
http://www.gowales.co.uk/en/graduate/index.html

Inland Revenue
http://www.hmrc.gov.uk/index.htm

Internships in the USA
www.aipt.org/

Library facilities away from your own university
http://www.access.sconul.ac.uk/

Money management
http://www.whataboutmoney.info/student_money/england/

Money made clear
Financial Service Authority Money Made Clear
www.fsa.gov.uk/guides

Mountbatten Scheme
www.mountbatten.org

National Council for Work Experience
For a wide range of information and contact points.
www.work-experience.org

Sites for placement opportunities
www.doctorjob.co.uk/workexperience
www.justjobsfor4students.co.uk
www.fledglings.net/
www.milkround.com

Prospects
For information and sources on graduate job opportunities.
www.prospects.ac.uk

Rate My Placement
www.ratemyplacement.co.uk

Shell STEP Summer Placements
www.step.org.uk

Working Abroad
www.workingabroad.org

Bibliography

Baxter, L., Hughes, C., and Tight, M. (2001) *How to Research*. Buckingham: Open University Press.

Becker, H. (1986) *Writing for Social Scientists*. Chicago: University of Chicago Press. (Cited in M. Easterby-Smith, R. Thorpe, and A. Lowe (2003) *Management Research*. London: SAGE.)

Belbin, R.M. (1981) *Management Teams: Why they Succeed or Fail*. Oxford: Heinemann.

Belbin Associates, UK Team-Note Descriptions.

Cameron, S. (2005) *The MBA Handbook*. Harlow: FT/Prentice-Hall.

CBI (2007) 'Shaping up for the future: the business vision for education and skills'. Report. London: CBI.

CBI/Pertemps (2007) *Employment Trends Survey*. London: CBI.

Chartered Institute of Personnel and Development (CIPD) (2008) Competency and competency frameworks Factsheet, November. http://www.cipd.co.uk/subjects/lrnanddev/designdelivery/otjtrain.htm?IsSrchRes=1 (accessed 7 March 2009).

Clutterbuck, D. (2004) *Everyone Needs a Mentor*, 4th edn. London: CIPD.

Easterby-Smith, M., Thorpe, R., and Lowe, A. (2003) *Management Research: An Introduction*. London: SAGE.

Gill, J. and Johnson, P. (1991) *Research Methods for Managers*. London: Paul Chapman.

Goleman, D. (1998) *Working with Emotional Intelligence*. London: Bloomsbury.

Hart, C. (2003) *Doing a Literature Review: Releasing the Social Science Research Imagination*. London: SAGE.

Heaton, N., McCracken, M. and Harrison, J. (2008) 'Graduate recruitment and development: sector influence on a local market/regional economy', *Education and Training*, 50(4): 276–88.

Honey, P. and Mumford, A. (2006) *The Learning Styles Questionnaire, 80-item version*. Maidenhead: Peter Honey.

Honey, P. and Mumford, A. (1986) *The Manual of Learning Styles*. Maidenhead: Peter Honey.

Huczynski, A.A. and Buchanan, D.A. (2007) *Organizational Behaviour*. Harlow: Pearson Education Ltd.

Janis, I. (1972) *Victims Group Think*. Boston, MA: Houghton-Mifflin.

Kaplan, R. and Norton, D. (1992) 'The balanced scorecard – measures that drive performance', *Harvard Business Review*, Jan–Feb: 71–9.

Kennedy, C. (2002) *Guide to the Management Gurus*. London: Random House.

Kolb, D.A., Rubin, I.M. and MacIntyre, J.M. (1984) *Organizational Psychology*, 4th edn. Englewoods Cliffs, NJ: Prentice-Hall.

Kotter, J. (1995) 'Leading change: why transformation efforts fail', *Harvard Business Review*, March–April.

Lambert Review of Business–University Collaboration (2003) *Final Report*, December. London: HMSO.

Maylor, H. (2003) *Project Management*. Harlow: Pearson Education.

Mintzberg, H. (1975) *The Nature of Managerial Work*. New York: Harper Row.

Murray, R. (2008) 'Writing anywhere, any time: 'snacking', 'retreating', and 'advancing' in academic writing'. 12th Writing Development in Higher Education Conference, 25–27 June, University of Strathclyde, Glasgow.

People Management (2008) *'Partnership, Working is key to improving graduate skills'. People Management*, 15 May: 14.

Rankin, N. (2004) 'The new prescription for performance: the eleventh competency benchmarking survey', *Competency & Emotional Intelligence Benchmarking Supplement 2004/2005*. London: IRS.

Salorey, P. and Mayer, J.D. (1989) 'Emotional intelligence', *Imagination, Cognition and Personality*, 9(3): 185–211.

Saunders, M., Lewis, P., and Thornhill, A. (2003) *Research Methods for Business Students*. Essex: Pearson.

Smith, A. (ed) (1819/1999) *The Wealth of Nations*, Books IV–V. London: Penguin.

Swain, H. (2008) The art of work experience. *The Guardian*, 27 May.

The South West of England Regional Development Agency, Graduates 4 Business http://www.southwestrda.org.uk/what-we-do/innovation/working/graduates4 business.shtm (accessed 7 March 2009).

Tuckman, B. (1965) 'Development sequences in small groups', *Psychological Bulletin*, 63(6): 384–99.

Universum (2006) Data from research conducted by Universum, used with permission via www.universumglobal.com

Index

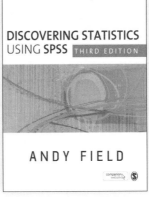
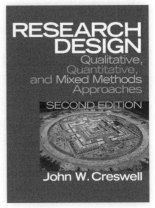

Supporting researchers for more than forty years

Research methods have always been at the core of SAGE's publishing. Sara Miller McCune founded SAGE in 1965 and soon after, she published SAGE's first methods book, *Public Policy Evaluation*. A few years later, she launched the Quantitative Applications in the Social Sciences series – affectionately known as the 'little green books'.

Always at the forefront of developing and supporting new approaches in methods, SAGE published early groundbreaking texts and journals in the fields of qualitative methods and evaluation.

Today, more than forty years and two million little green books later, SAGE continues to push the boundaries with a growing list of more than 1,200 research methods books, journals, and reference works across the social, behavioural, and health sciences.

From qualitative, quantitative and mixed methods to evaluation, SAGE is the essential resource for academics and practitioners looking for the latest in methods by leading scholars.

www.sagepublications.com